Beyond Breaking the Glass

A Spiritual Guide to Your Jewish Wedding

Rabbi Nancy H. Wiener, D.Min.

2010 09 08 07 06 05 04 03 02 2001   10 9 8 7 6 5 4 3 2 1

LIBRARY OF CONGRESS CATALOGING-IN-PUBLICATION DATA

Wiener, Nancy H., 1958-
  Beyond breaking the glass : a spiritual guide to your Jewish wedding
/ by Nancy H. Wiener.
    p. cm.
  ISBN 0-88123-097-9 (pbk.)
  1. Marriage customs and rites, Jewish. 2. Marriage--Religious
aspects--Judaism. 3. Reform Judaism--Customs and practices.   I.
Title.
  BM713 .W54 2001
  296.4'44--dc21

               2001017215

Grateful acknowledgement is made for permission to print the photographs
in this volume: photographer Trix Rosen © 1994, cover and pgs. xiii, 28, 30,
33, 35, 39, 42, 44, 48, 55, 62, 63, 67, 68, 72, 75, 85, 87, 95, 96, 98, 99, 131,
136; courtesy of the Library of the Jewish Theological Seminary of America, pgs. 7, 97; photographer Jose Ypes, pgs. 4, 34; Judith Tax and Nancy Wiener,
pgs. 1, 10, 13, 23, 32, 46, 65, 69, 70, 101, 102, 113, 122, 130; Jill Cowan and
Dan Wiener, title page and pg. 21; Gary Kiss and Gary Chimkin, pgs. 83, 118;
Ora Prochovnick and Rena Frantz, pgs. 47 (photo by Tala Brandeis), 119 (photo
by Jon Prochovnick); Hilary Zaid and Lauren Augusta, pg. 31 (photo by Bob
Ross); Rachel Kaufman and Leslie Snyder, pgs. 57, 106; Jackie and Jerry Lan-
genthal, pg. 79 (photo by JoVon Photography); Beth and Eric Jacobson, pg.
29; Barry Nostradamus Sher and Iris Korman, pg. 107 (photo by Alan Perl-
man); Nicole Bloom & Susan Swigart, pg. 93; Gary Pokras, pg. 109 (wedding
booklet).

Designed by BARRY NOSTRADAMUS SHER

CCAR Press
355 Lexington Avenue
New York, NY 10017
www.ccarpress.org

To Abbe Tiger and
Rabbi Julie Ringold Spitzer (z"l)

Their holy love was cause for all to rejoice

Contents

ACKNOWLEDGMENTS   xi

PREFACE   xiii

CHAPTER ONE   1
Mah Nishtanah: **What Makes This Different?**
Liberal Judaism's Distinctive Approach

An Overview   1

   Informed Jewish Decision-Making and You   1

   An Evolutionary View of Jewish History
   and Customs   2

   Judaism: An Ongoing Conversation—
   Responding to Ever-Changing Circumstances   5

   Reform Jewish Decision-Making:
   A Model to Consider   8

Contemporary Considerations   12

   Remarriage   12

   Same-Sex Marriage   13

CHAPTER TWO   15
A Holy Relationship

So, What Does All of This Have to
Do With Your Wedding?   15

How Have Jewish Weddings Evolved?   16

What Innovations Did the Reform Movement Introduce?   21

What is the Meaning of Your *Kiddushin* in the Contemporary Reform Community?   23

CHAPTER THREE   **27**
A Holy Transformation: Your *Kiddushin*

On the Day of Your *Kiddushin*   27

Beginning the Ceremony   28

    The Wedding Canopy / *Chuppah*   28

    Arriving at the *Chuppah*   33

    Circling   36

Betrothal Ceremony / *Kiddushin-Erusin*   39

    Welcome / Blessing of Welcome   40

    Blessing for Wine   40

    Blessing of Betrothal / *Birkat Erusin*   41

The *Ketubah*   43

    Reading Your *Ketubah*   45

    Signing Your *Ketubah*   46

Marriage Ceremony / *Nisuin-Chuppah*   46

    Vows and Rings   46

    The Wedding Address   52

    Seven Blessings / *Sheva B'rachot*   52

    Breaking a Glass   55

    The Pronouncement   58

Additional Blessings   59

    Shehecheyanu   59

    The Priestly Blessing / *Birkat Kohanim*   60

Some Pre-Ceremony Rituals   61

    Fasting   61

    Veiling / *B'deken*   62

    Tisch   65

Time Alone After the Ceremony / *Yichud*   66

Involving Friends and Relatives in the Ceremony   68

CHAPTER FOUR   **71**
A Holy Context: The Non-Ritual Elements

Creating a Holy Context   71

Planning With Intention / *Kavanah*   77

Engaging Clergy   78

    A Modern Jewish Phenomenon   78

    Availability and Fees   80

    Choosing Clergy   80

Choosing a Date   84

    Considering Your Personal Calendar   84

    Considering the Jewish Calendar   85

    Considering Convenience   92

Choosing a Location   92

The Wedding Party   95

The Reception   96

    Rejoicing and Recognition   96

    Tzedakah: Sharing Your
    Good Fortune With Others   100

    Food, Music and Photographic Mementos   101

Cost   105

Clothing   106

A Wedding Booklet   108

CHAPTER FIVE   **110**
A Holy Process: Personal and Spiritual Preparation

Setting Time Aside Before Your *Kiddushin*   110

Gaining Clarity About Your Relationship   111

    T'nai-im   112

    Getting or Making a *Ketubah*   117

Some Preparatory Customs   122

    Aufruf   122

    Mikveh   125

    Henna   127

    Food and Music   129

    Remembering the Past   131

CHAPTER SIX   **133**
Interfaith Marriage Ceremonies

The Reform Movement's Stance   133

Your Shared History of
Religious Decision-Making   134

Religious Decision-Making and Your Wedding   137

Choosing an Officiant   139

APPENDICES 141

I. Ceremony Checklist 141

II. Planning Time Line 144

III. *Chuppot* 151

IV. *Ketubot* 153

V. Vow Variations 154

VI. *Sheva B'rachot* Variations 157

VII. Blessing After Meals /
Birkat HaMazon for Weddings 175

VIII. Resources in the Reform Movement 183

Acknowledgments

I am grateful:

to my parents, who have provided me with a vibrant example of a long-term, loving, committed relationship;

to my *chevruta*, Rabbis Ellen Lippmann and Sue Oren, who have engaged me and nurtured me intellectually, emotionally and spiritually for the last seven years;

to the many with whom I have worked prior to their weddings, most especially Rich and Stephanie, and Alma and Brian, who read and provided invaluable suggestions about the manuscript;

to my colleagues and my students at Hebrew Union College–Jewish Institute of Religion, who have taught me and continue to teach me every day about life and love.

Finally, there are no words to express my gratitude to Judith Tax, my beloved, my life partner, my spouse. Daily she reminds me of the power of love and devotion. With her undying faith in me, her support and love, her keen eye for detail, as well as her exceptional editorial skills, my research and ideas were transformed into a book.

I join with the CCAR Press in gratefully acknowledging the following who generously permitted me to quote from the works cited:

SHEVA B'RACHOT VARIATION NO. 1: Rabbi Joan S. Friedman

SHEVA B'RACHOT VARIATION NO. 2: Rabbi Lester Polonsky, Educational Director, Temple Avodah, Oceanside, NY

SHEVA B'RACHOT VARIATION NOS. 3, 4: Rabbi Denise Eger, as adapted from "Sheva B'rachot" by Daniel Siegel in *The New Jewish Wedding:* Anita Diament (Summit Books, copyright © 1986)

SHEVA B'RACHOT VARIATION NOS. 5, 6: Rabbi Leila Gal Berner

SHEVA B'RACHOT VARIATION NO. 7: Rabbi Stacy Offner

SHEVA B'RACHOT VARIATION NO. 8: Rabbi Lisa Edwards and Tracey Moore, including contributions by Yaffa Weisman (Hebrew texts), Susan Silverman, Reena Kling and Miriam Bronstein

HUC PRESS: from *The Jew in the Medieval World* by Jacob Rader Marcus, copyright © 2000

JEWISH PUBLICATION SOCIETY: English translation of Deuteronomy 25 from *The Torah,* copyright © 1962, 1967

Every effort has been made to ascertain the owners of copyrights for the selections used in this volume. The Conference will be pleased, in subsequent editions, to correct any inadvertent errors or omissions that may be pointed out.

Preface

Mazal Tov! You've found the person with whom you would like to spend a lifetime. You've shared your dreams, hopes, expectations and the values you both uphold. And now, you are

contemplating the details of the day that will mark for you, your families and your friends the formation of a new family, with the two of you at its center.

People often begin their discussions of their wedding by focusing on the number of guests, the degree of formality, the time of year it will be held, the person who will officiate. In doing so, they frequently end up feeling unfocused and distanced from the extraordinary fact that they are two people who have fallen in love with each other and who are planning to make a life together.

Celebrating and affirming your love is important. You will remember this day for the rest of your lives. What do you want it to stand for? What do you want it to be remembered for? What does your relationship mean to you? What about your relationship is distinctive? What about your relationship is worthy of celebration and recognition? In what ways can family and friends enhance your celebration?

Understanding the answers to these questions can help you gain clarity and insight into the small and large details that will make your wedding most meaningful for you and for all those who join you on your wedding day.

You do not need to face all of these important questions alone. The clergy officiating at your wedding will be able to help you.

This book introduces you to and leads you through a process of liberal Jewish decision-making. It provides you with possibilities for giving your wedding special meaning, by offering a framework within which to plan the ceremonial, celebratory and practical aspects of your wedding. It gives an overview of a wide variety of wedding forms and customs practiced by Jews through the centuries and explains principles that have guided liberal Judaism in its reinterpretations. This book also describes some of the ways that Jewish weddings, and most recently liberal Jewish weddings, have responded to ever-evolving family configurations. Finally, the appendices enumerate a host of liberal Jewish alternatives for your wedding ceremony, as well as some of the resources in the broader community that can help transform your wedding day into a special one imbued with both personal and spiritual significance.

Chapter One

Mah Nishtanah: What Makes This Different?
Liberal Judaism's Distinctive Approach

An Overview

Informed Jewish Decision-Making and You

Welcome to the world of informed Jewish decision-making!

To be a liberal Jew is to live in a world of choices. To be a liberal Jew is to be held responsible for your actions. To be a liberal Jew is to strive to make every aspect of your life a reflection of your values. To be a liberal Jew is to believe that you are inextricably linked to your ancestors, yet bound to the

contemporary Jewish community, responsible for transmitting a meaningful and responsive Judaism to generations to come. To be a liberal Jew is to base your choices upon knowledge of Jewish traditions and history, contemporary knowledge and circumstances, and personal experience.

All actions have implications and convey meanings. They are connected with the past, the present and the future. The choices we make speak volumes about who we are, what we value and how we perceive the world. Every ritual with which we mark our life's transitions can communicate something about the values held and promoted by the communities of which we are a part.

You are now on a threshold, about to embark on a wonderful journey that will lead to your wedding. The many choices you will make about your wedding have the potential to express the meaning of your connections to each other, your families and friends, and the larger Jewish community. Take time to consider carefully the options presented throughout this book. The decisions you make can transform the formality of a tired or obscure ritual into a special, personally meaningful, sacred experience for you.

An Evolutionary View of Jewish History and Customs

Imagine a world that has never changed. Imagine a people whose customs have never been altered. Imagine a language that has never evolved. Is such a thing possible? Not in the world that we inhabit. No part of the natural world remains forever unchanged. Every people's customs have responded to changes in climate, leadership, locale and other influences. Every language's vocabulary and syntax have changed over time.

The Jewish people has a history that goes back more than 3,000 years. We trace our origins to the Fertile Crescent. For centuries, we all lived in one homeland. Then, with the rise and fall of various invading empires, most of us were forcibly scattered all over the world. Thus, for over 2,500 years, we have not lived together in one place; instead, we have lived as members of a cultural and religious minority, among the many other peoples of the earth.

Which of our original traditions have remained? How have our customs changed? How has our language evolved?

From our earliest beginnings, Jews have adapted to ever-changing circumstances. Since the first Israelites were exiled from their land more than 2,500 years ago, there has not been a period in history in which the practices, interpretations and languages of all Jews everywhere were identical. How could they be? Our people's understandings of ourselves and the world, our interpretations of sacred texts, and our customs and practices, all evolved in response to the cultures to which we were exposed.

For most of our history, there was little contact among the Jewish communities scattered around the world. Therefore,

Jews in one locality were largely unaware of the daily lives of Jews elsewhere. The sparse information they did have came primarily from personal travelogues, reports transmitted orally among Jews or legal documents that referenced local beliefs and customs. Most Jews assumed that their local customs were shared by all Jews around the world; they believed that any differences were mere anomalies.

In the last centuries, with the communication revolution and the transplantation of Jews from around the world to countries in the West and to Israel, we have become aware of and have grown to appreciate the great diversity of customs and expression that, in reality, had long characterized world Jewry. And yet, somehow, despite the profound differences in practice and interpretation that exist, we Jews have managed to retain

a sense of a shared history as well as an enduring commitment to living lives of meaning as Jews.

Judaism: An Ongoing Conversation—
Responding to Ever-Changing Circumstances

Ours is not the first generation, only the most recent one, to embody this significant truth: It is possible for a people's concerns and ideals to endure, even while the means to express and enact them change. Every generation of Jews has taken the traditions it has received and has adapted them to make them meaningful and relevant for the world in which it has lived.

Living in a world radically different from that of biblical times, the rabbis living in Palestine from the second century B.C.E. to the end of the second century C.E. analyzed and interpreted the tradition they had received. They studied the Torah's laws and sought to make them intelligible and meaningful for themselves and their contemporaries. Their world view and their daily lives diverged so much from those of their ancestors that their text study led to intense debates and discussions. The teachings, practices and legal decisions they produced were eventually written down in a work known as the Mishnah. Their own generations and those that followed them, no matter where in the world they lived, studied their teachings and interpretations, known as the Oral Torah, along with the written Torah. Even so, those who studied the Mishnah did not see it as the final word; rather, they accepted it as a significant work by the best legal minds of the time.

The completion of the Mishnah gave rise to a new round of discussions and debates among scholars and teachers in the two largest Jewish communities of the time, Palestine and Babylonia. These two sets of scholars and rabbis had the same starting points (the Torah and the Mishnah), yet the nature and content of their discussions, as well as their decisions, often diverged significantly. Each community produced its own compilation of study

and discussion of case law, known as Talmud. The two resulting Talmuds (Babylonian and Jerusalem) reflect each community's unique environment and daily concerns. Together, the two Talmuds provide us with a window into these very different worlds, while clearly illustrating the similar processes of decision-making that both communities employed.

The importance and centrality of this process of decision-making—valuing the received tradition while interpreting and defining its meaning and application through the lens of contemporary circumstances and knowledge—has so dominated Jewish life and learning that great scholars and rabbis of subsequent generations have always picked up and elaborated on the debates of their predecessors. They literally continued the discussion by offering their own commentaries, interpretations and observations about the practices and customs of their own times and localities alongside the texts they had inherited. When new cases or circumstances arose, the local rabbi first consulted the Jewish legal literature; then he either rendered his own opinion or wrote to the most respected rabbis of the time for help in adjudicating the case. Today we have copies of such questions and answers (Responsa, or in Hebrew, *sh'eilot ut'shuvot*) from

the past thousand years, and new ones are still being written. For example, a contemporary question, such as "What does Jewish law say about organ transplantation?" can generate multiple answers, each reflecting the interpretations, customs, state of technology, etc., of the particular rabbi or community from which it comes. In addition, if a group of rabbis, rather than a single rabbi, is consulted as a body, the response will often contain a split decision, enumerating both majority and minority opinions. In a traditional community, the local rabbi determines which of these decisions is binding for his community. In the Reform community, all such rabbinic decisions are considered informative and instructive, but none is binding on the community as a whole. Ultimately, each Reform Jew has the right and responsibility to engage in informed decision-making.

Every generation of Jews recognizes itself to be a link in the "chain of tradition," respecting the past and building on it to create the future. Our dual responsibility is to understand and value what we have inherited and to probe its meaning and application for our own time and place.

Reform Jewish Decision-Making: A Model to Consider

Reform Judaism began in the early nineteenth century in Germany. At that time, with the rise of nation-states and national identities, Jews were offered a new status in many emerging countries—equal citizenship. This major transition became known as "Jewish Emancipation." With Emancipation, Jews for the first time enjoyed access to education, professions, trades, land ownership, military service, etc. No longer forced to live as a people apart from the indigenous populations, they had new opportunities to live, study and work alongside non-Jews and to embrace and contribute to non-Jewish culture.

This world of new opportunities engendered a range of responses among Jews. Some rejected the non-Jewish world entirely. Others rejected the Jewish world—its teachings, customs and mores—deeming them incompatible with the new world that lay open before them. The early German Reformers believed that neither extreme response was necessary. They sought to find new forms for Jewish expression, both ceremonial and personal, that would enable Jews to simultaneously embrace their two identities, as Jews and as members of the societies and countries in which they lived. This revolutionary idea, introduced by the nineteenth-century Reform Movement, has become normative for most subsequent generations of Jews throughout the world.

The early Reformers asked new questions about Judaism and Jewish customs, reflecting their *zeitgeist*. They sought to isolate the abiding values and teachings of Judaism and to find meaningful and aesthetically and culturally acceptable ways of expressing them in the modern world. They believed that the essence of Judaism was ethical monotheism; they affirmed the existence of a creative power in the universe, the dignity of all human beings, and the human obligation to care about and take responsibility for both humanity and the world; and they felt the writings of the Prophets best expressed these beliefs. The first Reform rabbis undertook the enormous task of reviewing the laws,

customs and practices they had inherited in light of these beliefs. From their perspective, only some of the laws remained adequate reflections of Judaism's core values and teachings. Therefore, there were three approaches they adopted when an inherited law or practice conflicted with their understanding of Judaism. One approach was to try to make it relevant through reinterpreting it. Another approach was to develop a new custom that they understood as compatible with both Judaism's teachings and contemporary sensibilities. A third approach was to discard the practice entirely, deeming it archaic or non-authoritative for their generation.

Today, Reform Jews continue the process of studying Jewish laws and customs to determine their importance and place in the contemporary world. We understand that times change, as do people, and that the decisions of one generation may not speak to the next. We believe that all Jews, not just clergy and other communal officials, can contribute to and participate in the exciting, dynamic tradition they have inherited. To do so is no simple task. To be responsibly engaged with our tradition, we must first become familiar with Jewish beliefs and practices as they have evolved, and then make informed choices about how we as individuals and members of our communities will express ourselves as Jews. Building on the prophetic tradition and grappling with the realities of our contemporary world, we continue to expand upon the legacy of our forebears. Their novel approach to Emancipation made our lives as Jews and citizens possible. Their emphasis was on becoming citizens while remaining Jews; our emphasis has shifted to becoming informed and positively identified Jews while remaining fully engaged citizens. We have reembraced specifically Jewish understandings

of the world while retaining our commitment to humanity and the world. Today, in addition to the values we inherited, we affirm two additional significant values. All Jews, regardless of gender, religion of birth, prior affiliation or personal observance, deserve access to Jewish learning, ritual and leadership. Also, all Jews, regardless of family configuration or sexual orientation, are full particpants in communal life.

Whether you are planning your first marriage, remarriage or same-sex marriage, each of you will be confronting many of the same questions, concerns and issues. You will be engaging in the same process of decision-making, though your hierarchy of considerations will reflect your particular circumstances. Before continuing with your shared experiences, it is important to highlight aspects of liberal Judaism's unique approach to remarriage and same-sex ceremonies.

Contemporary Considerations

Remarriage

Liberal Judaism recognizes civil divorce as binding, and its clergy may perform a remarriage for any Jew who has a valid civil divorce document. Clergy in more traditionally observant communities require a Jewish divorce document (*get*) as well, in order to be able to officiate at a remarriage. Orthodox rabbis question the status of children born to remarried women who have not received a valid religious divorce. To avoid problems in the future, some liberal Jews, therefore, seek traditional Jewish divorces as well as civil ones. Discuss this very complex matter with the clergy who will officiate at your ceremony for help in deciding how you want to proceed.

Same-Sex Marriage

In recent decades an increasing number of liberal clergy have been officiating at ceremonies for gay and lesbian couples. Reform and Reconstructionist Judaism have officially rejected traditional Judaism's long-standing discriminatory attitudes and laws affecting gay men and lesbians. These movements are committed to reaching out to gay and lesbian Jews, welcoming individuals, couples and families with children to join their con-

gregations and to participate fully in the life of their communities. Consistent with its enduring commitment to social justice, Reform lay leaders and clergy have gone on record in support of the civil legalization of gay and lesbian marriage. The Central Conference of American Rabbis (CCAR), the Reform Movement's rabbinic organization, has passed a resolution stating that "the relationship of a Jewish, same gender couple is worthy of affirmation through appropriate Jewish ritual." The American Conference of Cantors, the Reform Movement's cantorial organization, has passed a similar resolution. These resolutions also recognize that each community and each member of the clergy has the right and the obligation to decide about officiation at religious ceremonies for gay and lesbian couples—leading, as always, to a wide variety of responses.

Chapter Two

A Holy Relationship

So, What Does All of This Have to Do With Your Wedding?

A great deal, if the concerns and approach of the Reform Movement and other liberal Jewish movements resonate with you. As a contemporary liberal Jew, you are likely to have mixed responses to aspects of the traditional Jewish wedding ritual. Some of it may speak as little to you and your world view as it did to the early Reformers, while other parts may be particularly meaningful or relevant to you. Since the middle of the nineteenth century, the Reform Movement has responded to a perceived gap between its world view and values and the traditional wedding ritual by reinterpreting the wedding, reworking and at times even disregarding certain long-standing customs and creating new liturgy. In fact, we are still actively engaged in this process today.

So that you can make informed choices about how you want to approach your wedding, a little background on Jewish weddings will be helpful.

How Have Jewish Weddings Evolved?

No wedding ceremony is ever described in the Torah. In the language of the Torah, men "took" women, and then they had offspring. Women were holdings of men, along with all other property. A woman's virginity and capacity to bear children determined her value. The Torah's main concerns had to do with men's having sexual relations with "available" women, i.e., women upon whom no other man had a legal claim. In this way, no man defiled another man's property, and the members of a man's household, women and children, were always easy to determine, for paternity was clear.

The world of the Torah, and part of the Jewish world well into the twentieth century, was polygamous. Men had multiple wives and concubines in order to "perpetuate their seed." The continuity of the male line was so important that the Torah even required a childless widow to marry her deceased husband's brother so that the family's "seed" would continue.

כי ישבו אחים יחדו ומת אחד
מהם ובן אין לו לא תהיה אשת
המת החוצה לאיש זר יבמה יבא
עליה ולקחה לו לאשה ויבמה
והיה הבכור אשר תלד יקום על
שם אחיו המת ולא ימחה שמו
מישראל

When brothers dwell together and one of them dies and leaves no son, the wife of the deceased shall not be married to a stranger, outside the family. Her husband's brother shall unite with her: take her as his wife and perform the levir's duty. The first son that she bears shall be accounted to the dead brother, that his name may not be blotted out in Israel.

As we learn from the Mishnah, by two thousand years ago certain betrothal and marriage laws and customs were already normative in Jewish communities. A Jewish male, his parents or a designated agent publicly announced his intention to "acquire" a wife. A betrothal became valid when a formula of betrothal was recited and something of value was given to the girl or woman or her representative as a sign of acquisition—in Hebrew, *kinyan*. From the time of the betrothal, the girl or woman belonged to her betrothed and was sexually set aside for him. She could not have sexual relations until she was married, and then only with her betrothed. (In contrast, a man could have other sexual partners, even other wives!) She was set aside for a specific holy purpose: procreation. The rabbis viewed this act of setting aside as conceptually akin to setting something aside for God. Thus, another name for the process of betrothal was *kiddushin*, meaning to set aside for an exclusively holy purpose.

As with other acquisitions, "ownership" of a girl or woman as a wife was valid when accompanied by a written document, a *ketubah*. The *ketubah* stipulated the conditions upon which the agreement of acquisition was made: the female's prior marital status and virginity; the property which she brought into the marriage; and the property to which she would have a legal claim in the case of divorce or widowhood. (Imagine: Over two thousand years ago, when there was little notion of a woman's living independently, Jewish law recognized the need to provide for her continued financial maintenance so that her returning to her parents' or sibling's home would not become a financial burden!)

The ancient laws of acquisition for "movable objects" required a person to demonstrate ownership by pulling, lifting or carrying the acquired object or transferring it to his domain. Thus, the common Hebrew word for marriage, *nisuin*, comes from the root meaning "to lift" or "to carry." (Take a moment to consider the probable origins and implications of our quaint old custom of a new husband's carrying his bride over the threshold of his home!) *Kinyan* was completed at *nisuin*, when the bride was transferred (carried) to her husband's house. Jewish marriage was clearly a legal transaction of acquisition.

The "traditional" Jewish wedding ceremonies that evolved over the centuries since then have been the product of our age-old decision-making process. They contained elements of practices mentioned in the Mishnah, elaborations upon those practices and specific prayers enumerated in the Talmuds, and variations in customs that Jews living in different places adopted as their own. At their core, though, all pre-modern Jewish weddings shared a set of basic assumptions: 1) Women were not independent beings—they were members of one man's household; 2) The actions that made a girl or woman a man's wife were all initiated and enacted by men—that is, she became a man's wife when he gave her a written document and a token of specified value, and took her to bed; 3) Procreativity was the major reason for a man to take a wife—companionship was a welcome, but not required, perquisite. As a legal transaction, *kiddushin* needed two male witnesses to sign the *ketubah;* as a religious ritual, a *minyan* (a prayer quorum of ten) was needed. Custom eventually combined these and it became normative to have both the two witnesses and a *minyan* at a wedding.

Over time, the first stage of the legal transaction of betrothal, *kinyan/kiddushin*—the acts of acquisition and setting aside—became much more formal. It was marked by the preparation and signing of a legally witnessed document stipulating specific conditions to be met, such as the date and place of the nuptials and the amount to be paid by each family prior to the actual wedding. The completion of this legally binding document was accompanied by a festive meal and blessings, including a special betrothal blessing known as *Birkat Erusin.* The betrothal ceremony became known as *kiddushin/erusin.*

Originally, the actual marriage ceremony, *nisuin*, was very brief. The man gave the girl or woman a token (for many centuries, among Western Jewish communities, it was most often a ring) that marked her as his. He stated that he was taking her as his wife in accordance with Jewish law. The rabbi and/or other men in attendance offered special blessings, known as *Birkat Nisuin*, following which the couple drank wine. (The Talmuds offer different formulations for *Birkat Nisuin*. Eventually, it became normative for seven blessings to be offered.) Family and community then celebrated the *nisuin* with a festive meal. The marriage became legal and binding once the couple had had sexual relations and it was clear that the bride's state of virginity had been as promised.

During the Middle Ages, in many communities, particularly in the West, the separate ceremonies of betrothal and marriage were fused into one, with two discrete parts. The single ceremony became known as *kiddushin/nisuin*, or *kiddushin* for short. Some rabbis and historians suggest that the new single ceremony represented a response to the economic strain imposed by having two celebrations. Others suggest that it reflected the precariousness of Jewish life in the Middle Ages, creating pressure to hasten the marriage process. Finally, others suggest that it was a way of reducing the couples' temptation to have sexual contact between their betrothal and their wedding.

Some of these traditional Jewish practices are still maintained today. Some communities still have arranged marriages. Many still utilize traditional legal documents drawn up by the men upon whom the woman is dependent (i.e., her father and her husband-to-be) and witnessed and signed by males only. At these weddings a woman receives her marriage document, receives a token (but does not give one), is assured by her husband that she is being married according to Jewish customs (but says nothing herself), and is legally wed once the marriage is consummated. She remains married until her husband dies or until *he* grants *her* a divorce. It is exclusively the man's desires and actions that create or dissolve a marriage.

What Innovations Did the Reform Movement Introduce?

While this was the wedding ceremony that the early Reformers inherited, it was not what they retained. These men were students of the ideologies and teachings of the European Enlightenment and Romanticism. They functioned in a world in which well-educated and affluent members of European society valued romantic love and advocated equality for all people. In this new world, an increasing number of young, educated Jews were living apart from their families of origin prior to marriage; their love relationships were separate from the sphere of their parents' influence. They began to conceive of marriage as a contract into

which a couple freely entered, not a legal commercial transaction between families.

As a result, marriage was among the first rituals studied, analyzed and reworked by the early rabbis of the Reform Movement. Believing that the wedding ritual solemnized and blessed the bride's and groom's commitment to *each other*, rather than a commitment between the groom and the bride's father, they significantly changed the ceremony of *kiddushin*. The new ceremony highlighted both members of the couple as active participants. Groom *and* bride spoke to each other as they exchanged rings. Blessings were offered that reflected a gratitude for creation, a hope that the couple would have children and a hope that the couple would be happy. The use of a religious legal document became optional. If such a document was included, it was written in the vernacular, to be intelligible to those who signed it, and all references to "bride price" and virginity were expurgated from the text. From their radical egalitarian point of view, it was clear to the Reformers that any Jew, male or female, could sign the marriage document as a witness. Furthermore, concerned about the unilateral nature of traditional Jewish divorce, they decided to recognize civil divorces, not just religious divorces, as binding. These changes are considered normative among most liberal Jews today, but in the middle of the nineteenth century they were extraordinary innovations! They were the cause for much debate withi. eral circles, as well as great consternation and anger 1 non-liberal ones.

What is the Meaning of Your *Kiddushin* in the Contemporary Reform Community?

Today, in liberal Jewish circles, your *kiddushin* has a richness of meaning. It is a significant milestone in a process that the two of you began the day you met. The root of the word *kiddushin* means to take someone or  something that others might see as ordinary and to separate it out, to distinguish it, to elevate it for a holy purpose. For most other people, your beloved is "just another person." But for you, that is far from the case. In your eyes, in your heart, in your life, this seemingly ordinary individual is like no other you have ever known. And the relationship that you have with each other is unlike any you have ever known. You offer each other a unique fusion of emotional, spiritual and sexual intimacy. For some time now, in ways large and small, you have been setting each other apart and treating each other in ways that demonstrate the love, concern and commitment that has been growing between you.

is the basis for your *kiddushin*, your Jewish mar-
moment to formally set each other and your
apart. Publicly, you will stand in front of friends and
family and affirm the holiness, the sacred distinctiveness, of your
relationship. As equals, you will freely declare your current and
future commitment to one another.

Your *kiddushin* is so much more than a legal *transaction*,
so much more than a civil change of status; it is a spiritual and
personal *transformation*.

On the day of your *kiddushin*, you will promise to nurture and sustain your relationship. On that day, as well, you will
ask all those present to promise you that they will aid you, in
whatever ways they can, to nurture and sustain the hopes, dreams
and commitments you are making. Together, you can make the
day of your *kiddushin* cause for all of you and, according to our
tradition, especially for God, to rejoice.

As you prepare for your *kiddushin*, take time to reflect
on the ways you have set each other apart, and share them with
one another. Take time to consider the character traits you cher-
ish in each other. Take time to talk together about the values you
share, the meaning of your upcoming *kiddushin* for each of you,
and the ways it can reflect who you are as individuals and as
a couple. You can do this over a period of time, in several sittings,

but really take time to *do* it; you will be rewarded with a heightened appreciation of the love you share.

If this is the second time you are celebrating *kiddushin*, then, as you review your current relationship, be sure to share with each other the ways this relationship differs from your previous marriage(s) and how you have changed. It may seem self-evident to you, but articulating the "obvious" can lead to significant insights for both of you.

As contemporary, liberal Jews, you have a unique opportunity not available to earlier generations. You can decide whether you want your ceremony to be similar or identical to "normative" liberal *kiddushin,* and even whether or not you want to call your ceremony *kiddushin.* While throughout this book the word *kiddushin* will be used, you may feel that the term is too intimately bound with traditions and assumptions that you yourselves don't hold. Some couples have chosen to emphasize the holiness of their love by calling their ceremony *kiddush ahavah*—sanctification of love; others have emphasized the covenant or contract they are entering, calling their ceremony a *brit ahuvim / brit ahuvot* (covenant of lovers) or a *brit ahavah* (covenant of love). This is something to consider prior to selecting your officiant, so that you can work with someone who understands and respects the choices you have made.

As a gay or lesbian couple, you will find that some rabbis are comfortable with any choice you make; however, there will be others who are opposed to the use of the traditional *"kiddushin,"* reserving it exclusively for heterosexual marriage. For the clergy, and most especially for you, this is more than a matter of labels; it is a matter of meaning and message. Consider what choosing to ceremonially mark your relationship means to you, and how important it is to do so with recognizable and age-old forms or with innovative and distinctive elements. Once you gain clarity about this yourselves, you will be able to make decisions about more than a name for your ceremony—you will also be able to make informed choices about choreography, vows, blessings and the pronouncement you want to include.

Chapter Three

A Holy Transformation:
Your *Kiddushin*

On the Day of Your *Kiddushin*

During your *kiddushin* a remarkable transformation will occur. You will begin the ceremony as two individuals with shared hopes and dreams and visions. And miraculously, by the ceremony's conclusion, you will be a new entity, a new Jewish family!

You may ask: How does this happen? Exactly when does it happen? Who or what makes it happen?

It is impossible to pinpoint the exact moment you will know that you have been forever changed. Yet through this ceremony, generations of people have experienced such a transformation. At the ceremony, *you* will be the primary actors. Your friends and families will be the witnesses. The clergy will help make sure that everything is done exactly as you have planned, serving as facilitator(s)—in Hebrew, a *m'sadeir kiddushin* [male] or *m'saderet kiddushin* [female], the organizers of the *kiddushin*. The two of you will be engaged in a holy act, at a holy time. At this unique moment you will be affirming your covenant of love, the unique place you have set aside for each other in the life the two of you are establishing together. You will be looking back at the past, with an eye to the future that will be yours.

Today, Jews of European extraction still adhere, in large or small measure, to the ritual structure adopted in the Middle Ages. The following discussions of the different elements of the ceremony and of a variety of marital customs can help you make informed decisions about what you want for *your kiddushin.*

Beginning the Ceremony

The Wedding Canopy / Chuppah

At a Jewish ceremony, it is under the *chuppah,* the nuptial canopy, that the extraordinary transformation marked by

kiddushin traditionally occurs. Originally, a bride's arrival under the *chuppah* symbolized for her and the community at large her entrance into her husband's domain, her becoming a member of her husband's household. Today, from a liberal

egalitarian perspective, the *chuppah* is most commonly understood as a symbol of the new home that you are establishing together through your *kiddushin*.

In the grand scheme of Jewish history, the central place that the portable *chuppah* enjoys at a Jewish wedding is fairly recent, dating only from sometime in the sixteenth century! Nonetheless, today in America, most Jews and even many non-Jews recognize the *chuppah* as one of the most distinctive and enduring ritual objects and symbols of a Jewish wedding. As we explore below some of the meanings that the *chuppah* has had and some of the forms that it has taken, perhaps you will be inspired to look at the *chuppah* in new and meaningful ways.

Literally, *chuppah* means covering. This covering demarcates the holy space in which a Jewish couple affirms the sanctity of their relationship. In earlier times, when Jews often held weddings on market days, the *chuppah* was a physical means of distinguishing the special area in which the wedding ceremony would occur from the surrounding hubbub. In a very real sense, no matter where your wedding takes place, there will be inherent distractions for all who are present; the *chuppah* continues to focus attention upon you and the holy space in which your lives together will be transformed.

Chuppot (the Hebrew plural) have taken a wide variety of forms, from the canopied couches for brides and grooms of medieval Central Europe, to an article of the husband's clothing (such as a *tallit*) draped over the bride and groom, to an embroidered ark cover (*parochet,* in Hebrew); from a simple piece of silk, to velvet suspended on poles, to a bower of flowers. Unlike the case for many other Jewish ritual objects, there are no requirements for *chuppot.* Customarily, they have taken the form of a covering, serving as a portable roof. A large *chuppah* is  reminiscent of the nomadic tents used long ago by our Jewish ancestors, and is still used today in parts of the world. Such a tent roof with no walls might seem to lack form and strength, much like the new family and the new home you are establishing. However, such a tent is also flexible; it can adapt to variable circumstances and withstand harsh, abrupt changes that a more rigid structure might not. Moreover, as a symbol of your new home, your *chuppah* represents some of the qualities of your future life together: It is inhabited by you, surrounded by your family and friends, supported by representatives of the (religious) community to which you belong and protected by the sheltering presence of God; It can be filled with acts of love and kindness, a place in which guests are always welcome, as were the tents of our ancestors Abraham and Sarah.

Your *chuppah* may be of any size, so it is up to you to decide whether it will cover only you, or you and the clergy, or you and your immediate families, or you and your entire wedding party, etc. The options are  numerous, as are the meanings you are choosing to convey. To help figure out the right size for you, start by asking yourselves: What is the relationship between you and your new home, you and your family, you and your community? Agreeing on answers to these questions can serve as a practical guide to your decision regarding the size of your *chuppah*.

In some communities it is customary for the *chuppah* to be freestanding; in others, it is hand-held by members of the wedding party. In either case, it is considered an honor to be a symbolic or real *chuppah* holder. Some communities own *chuppot* that members can rent or borrow. Alternatively, many couples choose to make or buy their own, or ask family or friends to join in creating one for (or with) them. As a ceremonial object, it is intended to heighten the beauty of your marriage ceremony, to be a reflection of the Jewish custom of *hidur mitzvah,* meaning the embellishing of a holy act. Therefore, your *chuppah* can reflect your aesthetic sense; you can choose the design, the material, the decoration and the poles. There are many artists who design and make *chuppot,* either for or with the couple (see Appendix III). Take the time to think of ways to personalize this important ritual object.

One couple, for example, had worked in Africa and chose to use a cloth they had brought back with them for their *chuppah.* Ellen and Bill decided to use Ellen's mother's table cloth,

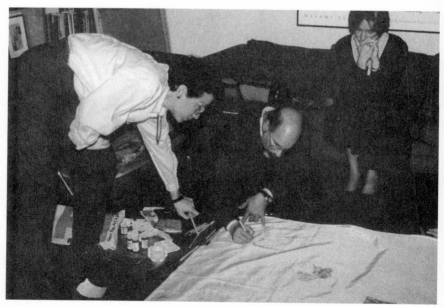

since family meals represented an important piece of the home they sought to establish. Judith and Nancy invited friends to come an hour before their ceremony to decorate their plain white silk *chuppah* with personal wishes in words and art.

Just one practical note: Make sure the poles you use are of sufficient height (a minimum of four to five feet, if hand-held; seven to eight feet if freestanding) to comfortably hang above the heads of those who will be standing under it!

Arriving at the Chuppah

The choreography at a Jewish wedding has always reflected the customs of the dominant culture of the country or locality in which the Jewish couple has lived, as well as the per-

sonal preferences of the family and the customs of the local Jewish community. Today, in America, we too have adopted wedding customs from the dominant culture, the Anglo-Saxon Christian world in which we live. None of these "mainstream" conventions are connected to the "Jewishness" or legality of your ceremony. In truth, Judaism has no rules, only customs, regarding processions and entrances.

And you can even choose to have no formal procession or entrance at all. Each option bears a different symbolic message; only you know what messages you wish to convey at the outset of your ceremony.

In parts of Muslim Africa, men on mules with guns and drums accompany the groom from the river, where he has bathed, to his home where the ceremony takes place, while singing and dancing women accompany the bride from the running water, where she has bathed, to the place of the ceremony. Throughout the Muslim Jewish world, it is customary for the groom to be treated as a sheik and for his friends to behave like members

of his court for a number of days prior to his wedding, when they then make up his entourage.

In medieval Persia, a crowd carrying torches illuminated the bridegroom's way to the bride's house, where the canopy was then erected. In medieval Egypt, there is a record of a bride's arriving with her entourage with sword in hand, wearing a helmet, while the groom and the other young men arrived wearing women's clothes, with henna on their nails! (We have no way of knowing whether this was a common practice or mere unique occurrence.) And in Eastern Europe, until the Second World War, it was customary for bride and groom to be escorted by musicians and friends from their homes to the site of their ceremony, inviting guests to join in the procession as it wended its way through the streets of the town.

At your ceremony, you can each be escorted by a parent or parents, either all the way to the *chuppah* or part way to it. Or you can choose to walk to the *chuppah* either separately or together. In some communities, one member of the couple is

escorted by the two fathers, while the other is escorted by the two mothers. Your entrances can be candlelit, and they can be accompanied by music. The possibilities are endless for what your procession can look like, what your roles in it might be, and whom you select to participate in it. Jon and Melanie had their guests' seats set up in a semicircle facing the center of the arc they created. They entered arm in arm toward a free-standing *chuppah*. Their parents stood outside the *chuppah*; their grandparents were seated nearby. Matt and Stephanie were danced in separately, led by chains of reveling friends who then held

f their *chuppah*. At Lee and Lisa's outdoor ceremony,
ed at the area where the *chuppah* stood riding
p an antique convertible. When they descended from
the car, each was accompanied the rest of the way by a special
person who had nurtured and sustained her, someone she identified as a non-biological, "spiritual" parent.

Circling

Peoples all around the world and from every era of history have believed that circles have magical powers. Many Jewish
folk customs, including those for marriage, reinforce this belief.
One custom, whose original form and meaning have been lost,
has the bride circling the space that she and her husband will
inhabit. Among the Jews of rural Muslim Africa, the bride, seated
on an animal, is led from the *mikveh* to her husband-to-be's
house; prior to the wedding blessings and feast, she is led in circles around the house. The number of circles she makes varies
from community to community.

Among most Western Jews, the practice of circling has
become incorporated into the public ceremony of *kiddushin* and
now takes place at the couple's symbolic home, the *chuppah*.
Law codes and writings from various Jewish communities and
eras mention differing numbers of circles, three and seven being
most common. In most descriptions of this custom, the bride

is not alone as she circles her husband; she is led around him by her mother, the rabbi or another significant member of the community.

Over the centuries, rabbis have attempted to find biblical and legal bases for this custom. Some trace it to a passage from the Book of Jeremiah (chapter 31, verse 22), in which Jeremiah suggests that in a future messianic time, relationships between men and women will be radically different. The image that he uses to express this is: "A woman will court a man," rather than the reverse. Because the Hebrew verb for courting can also mean "to go around," it became customary for the woman literally "to go around" the man. Another tradition locates the biblical basis for a woman's circling in the Song of Songs (chapter 8, verses 9 and 10), which likens a woman to a wall; various commentators believed that the wife's circling created a protective wall around her husband, keeping him from external temptation. Yet another explanation offered in communities in which three circles are the norm, is that each circle represents one of the three obligations a husband must fulfill toward his wife: sustenance, clothing and sexual relations. Jewish mystics, *kabbalists*, associate the number seven with wholeness or completion. As the earth revolved around the sun seven times to complete the Creation, so a bride revolves around her husband seven times to show that their marriage symbolically reenacts Creation.

Early Reform practice dispensed with this ritual altogether, viewing it as superstitious, non-egalitarian and inessential. However, today some couples are again choosing to include the tradition of circling in their ceremonies, reinterpreting it and refocusing it with modern understandings. Emily and Jeff found the notion of defining a protective circle around each other appealing. In some feminist circles the circling has become an act of empowerment, through which the woman delineates the sacred space of the union. Camille and Karen chose to share the circling, with each member of the couple circling the other an equal number of times, and then walking together to create a final circle together. Some couples also ascribe meanings to the circles by having biblical verses or poetic verses read as each circle is made. One choice is from Hosea (chapter 2, verses 21 and 22) which says: "I will betroth you to me forever; and I will betroth you to me in righteousness and justice, and in loyal love, and in mercy. And I will betroth you to me in faithfulness."

It is up to you to decide whether or not you want to include this custom; if you do, feel free to be creative in your adaptation of its symbolism. For example, Jason and Miriam chose to have each circle represent an emotion they brought into the safe and sacred space that they created through their union; with each circle, they acted out a different emotion.

The Betrothal Ceremony / *Kiddushin-Erusin*

Most Reform *kiddushin* retain vestiges of the originally separate ceremonies of betrothal and marriage. Often two separate cups of wine are blessed and drunk, one toward the beginning of the ceremony and the other toward its end. If you

choose to include these rituals, there is an opportunity for you to think creatively about the cups or glasses you will use. (These are not the ones you may break at the end!) You can choose cups that have special meaning for the two of you, such as family heirlooms, kiddush cups, glasses used by other family members at their

weddings, etc. Also, you may decide how many cups you want to use. There are several possibilities: You can each drink from a separate cup, or the two of you can share the same cup each time. Some couples like the symbolism of drinking from separate cups at the beginning of the ceremony and then filling a single (third) cup from their separate cups, from which they both drink at the end of the ceremony. The choice is yours.

Welcome / Blessing of Welcome

The ceremony will begin with some sort of official welcome. There are standard formulas some clergy like to use; these can be spoken or sung. However, many clergy are open to developing individualized blessings or greetings with you. Some couples also ask the clergy to include some brief remarks about the service and its symbols so that guests will understand what is taking place. Others choose, instead or in addition, to provide guests with a booklet containing explanations of rituals and customs, as well as the words to selected prayers (see "A Wedding Booklet" in Chapter Four).

Blessing for Wine

Wine is a symbol of joy in Judaism. We bless wine (the fruit of the vine) on all holidays and at all joyous occasions. The blessing for wine is very simple; it may be either recited or chanted. It says:

בָּרוּךְ אַתָּה יְיָ, אֱלֹהֵינוּ מֶלֶךְ הָעוֹלָם, בּוֹרֵא פְּרִי הַגָּפֶן.

Baruch atah Adonai, Eloheinu Melech haolam, borei p'ri hagafen.

Blessed are You, Adonai our God, Ruler of the Universe, who creates the fruit of the vine.

If you prefer to use grape juice at your *kiddushin*, the blessing is the same; it is still "the fruit of the vine!"

Blessing of Betrothal / Birkat Erusin

You may choose to have the clergy chant or recite an additional blessing of betrothal over the cup of wine which states:

בָּרוּךְ אַתָּה יְיָ, אֱלֹהֵינוּ מֶלֶךְ הָעוֹלָם, אֲשֶׁר קִדְּשָׁנוּ בְּמִצְוֹתָיו
(וְצִוָּנוּ עַל הָעֲרָיוֹת, וְאָסַר לָנוּ אֶת הָאֲרוּסוֹת,) וְהִתִּיר לָנוּ אֶת
הַנְּשׂוּאִים וְהַנְּשׂוּאוֹת לָנוּ עַל יְדֵי (חוּפָּה וְ) קִדּוּשִׁין. בָּרוּךְ אַתָּה
יְיָ, מְקַדֵּשׁ עַמּוֹ יִשְׂרָאֵל עַל יְדֵי (חֻפָּה וְ) קִדּוּשִׁין.

Blessed are You, Adonai our God, Ruler of the Universe, who has sanctified us with Your commandments (and has commanded us concerning forbidden connections, and has forbidden us those who are merely betrothed, but) [and] has allowed to us those lawfully married to us through *(chuppah* and) *kiddushin.* Blessed are You Adonai, our God, who sanctifies Your people Israel through *(chuppah* and) *kiddushin.*

This simple prayer affirms two distinct and important ideas. First, according to the Torah and later legal writings, sexual relations are forbidden among non-married family members; with the creation of a new family through marriage, such prohibitions are extended to include in-laws as well. Second, the only permitted sexual relations for a man (the prayer is written for men, about their relations with women) are those with a

woman he has married under a *chuppah* and with a specifically Jewish ritual, referred to in shorthand as *kiddushin.*

The early Reformers found aspects of this prayer objectionable. They removed in its entirety the reference to prohibited sexual relations and retained the final part that affirms the sanctity of marital relations consecrated through Jewish ritual. Some contemporary liberal Jews have again begun to include this prayer, but understand it to be addressed to both members of the couple. During their *kiddushin,* some couples wish to underscore sexual exclusivity as an essential piece of their marital relationship. Speak to your clergy about the numerous versions of this prayer from which you can choose, should you opt to include it in your ceremony. This blessing is entirely optional at a liberal *kiddushin.*

The *Ketubah*

Ketubah means "written document." Though it can refer to any written Jewish legal document, over time *ketubah* has come to be associated with a document signed immediately prior to a Jewish wedding. The text of a *ketubah* was originally prepared and signed by the fathers or agents of the bride- and the groom-to-be. The document was traditionally written in Aramaic (the *lingua franca* of Jews, and therefore the language of business transactions and literature for many centuries, beginning in the late biblical period). It attested to the bride's virginity, and stated the value that the groom or his family would pay for the bride, the amount of the dowry, the responsibilities of the husband for his wife's maintenance and welfare, the amount the bride would receive in the event of a divorce, and the fact that the ceremony would be in accordance with strict Jewish law and witnessed by two "kosher" males. The bride played no part in its preparation, and she did not sign it. To this day, in Orthodox Jewish communities, the *ketubah* is still the Aramaic document described above. And traditional Jewish legal courts continue to recognize it as legally binding.

Finding the economic aspects of this signed agreement objectionable, the first Reform rabbis did not require the traditional *ketubah* for their *kiddushin*. They introduced a *ketubah* written in the vernacular, so that both members of the couple and all those in attendance could understand it. As an expression of their commitment to egalitarianism, they allowed either male or female witnesses to sign it. References to the virginity of the bride were removed from the text, as were all references to money. It simply attested to the fact that a binding religious ceremony had occurred.

Some Reform clergy felt that it was unnecessary to have a specific Jewish marriage document at all. They reasoned that since Jews needed to register their marriages with the state, the civil license was sufficient to attest to the validity of the marriage. By the middle of the twentieth century, therefore, most

Reform Jews in the United States did not include a traditional Aramaic *ketubah* or any Jewish document in their wedding ceremony. If they used a Jewish certificate of any sort, the body of the text was written in English.

In recent years, the decision to include a *ketubah* has again become common in the liberal Jewish community, although it remains optional. Among today's Reform Jews, the *ketubah* is usually an expression of the couple's personal pledges to each other, and is often made into a beautiful piece of art (see

"Getting or Making a *Ketubah*" in Chapter Five). A *ketubah* is normative among gay and lesbian couples, who do not have a civil license attesting to their marital status. If you are celebrating your same-sex union, take time to plan together what you want to include in your *ketubah*. Will it enumerate those responsibilities and expectations that are assumed (correctly or erroneously) to accompany a civilly recognized marriage, i.e., those that come with "next-of-kin" status? Will it include specific commitments, financial and otherwise, that you wish to record in a witnessed document?

Reading Your Ketubah

When the separate betrothal and wedding ceremonies were fused, many Jewish communities adopted the custom of reading the *ketubah* aloud as a bridge or break between them. At today's traditional Jewish weddings, the *ketubah*, with its many clauses and conditions, is still read aloud in Aramaic. Until recent decades, Reform weddings rarely included the reading of a *ketubah*.

With the creation of liberal *ketubot* (the Hebrew plural) expressing the hopes and commitments of the new family being formed, many liberal Jewish couples are choosing to have their *ketubot* read aloud during their *kiddushin*. Sharing the contents of your *ketubah* with guests and witnesses allows everyone to gain a greater personal understanding of the meaning your *kid-dushin* has for you.

Signing Your Ketubah

Some couples choose to sign the document as part of the ceremony. Others follow the long-standing tradition of signing the *ketubah* immediately prior to the ceremony. If you follow the tradition of having two witnesses sign your *ketubah*, they should be Jews who are non-family members; they can be male or female. They may sign in English and/or in Hebrew. Some couples have 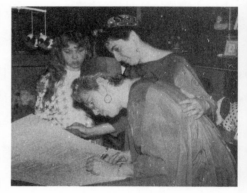 chosen to have everyone in attendance sign their *ketubah*. Most liberal *ketubot* are also signed by the members of the couple and the officiating clergy.

Marriage Ceremony / *Nisuin-Chuppah*

Vows and Rings

In parts of medieval Europe it was customary for the groom to place a large silver ring, intricately designed in the shape of a house, on his bride's index finger and say in Aramaic the words "Behold, you are consecrated to me with this ring, according to the laws of Moses and Israel." The bride gave him nothing and said nothing to him. And they were married. Over the centuries, the ring style, as well as the finger upon which the ring is placed, has varied. Some traditional communities maintain the custom of placing the ring on the bride's index finger to make it visible to all. In most liberal Jewish circles, the ring is placed directly onto the ring finger.

Some of the most extraordinary pieces of Jewish ritual art are rings designed for weddings. In some communities, one highly stylized ring (often in the shape of a house) was used during the ceremony, and another ring was worn as the permanent marriage token. As long as the permanent ring was a solid piece of precious metal whose weight and value

could be clearly determined (remember, this was a business transaction), it could have been used at any Jewish wedding in any part of Western, Central or Eastern Europe during the past thousand or more years. Replace the ring with a piece of cloth, expensive spices or other articles of specific value and you could be in a Jewish community from Asia, the Indian subcontinent, the Middle East or Africa in the same time period. As the groom placed the ring on the bride's finger, he recited words that identified the ring as a token of marriage. She neither gave him a comparable token nor made any verbal claims upon him.

Since contemporary liberal communities no longer recognize *kiddushin* as a business transaction, our *kiddushin* ceremonies allow for several variations in this part of the ceremony. For one thing, both partners can choose to give each other a token. Also, the choice of tokens has broad-ened considerably. Most liberal clergy accept any style of ring or any other object as the official token. In most traditional communities, however, a ring of one solid piece of metal is still the rule. The only limits, therefore, are set by your imaginations, tastes and the customs of your communities.

The token given is only a symbol, a material pledge, for the vows that are said. The traditional formulaic declaration is:

הֲרֵי אַתְּ מְקֻדֶּשֶׁת לִי בְּטַבַּעַת זוֹ כְּדַת מֹשֶׁה וְיִשְׂרָאֵל.

Harei at m'kudeshet li b'tabaat zo k'dat Moshe v'Yisrael.

This literally means:

> Behold, you are consecrated for/to me, with this ring, according to the religion/tradition of Moses and Israel.

Once again, this was originally said only by the man. However, in modern, egalitarian *kiddushin*, women also make a vow. Since Hebrew is a gender-based language, with most words (including nouns, pronouns, adjectives and verbs) indicating gender and number, the traditional phrase above must be modified if it is to be said to a man:

הֲרֵי אַתָּה מְקֻדָּשׁ לִי בְּטַבַּעַת זוֹ כְּדַת מֹשֶׁה וְיִשְׂרָאֵל.

Harei atah m'kudash li b'tabaat zo k'dat Moshe v'Yisrael.

Notice that the changes are made to indicate the person being spoken *to,* not the person speaking. Your clergy will ensure that you say the correct form, if these are the words you plan to use.

Let us take a few moments to consider the import of these words. *Harei at/atah* means "Behold, You! (Or, 'Pay attention!') Don't make a mistake. Take a look." Each member of the couple turns to the other and affirms, "You are the one to whom I am speaking." *M'kudeshet/mikudash li* comes from the same root as *kiddushin*. With these words you are saying to each other, in front of witnesses, "I am setting this relationship, and you, apart from all others, for myself. I will treat you differently from all others. I will see you as no others see you. And I will treat our relationship as holy." How does this happen? How can we be sure that this is your intent? *B'tabaat zo,* "By this ring" that you give. And lest anyone think that this is not a serious matter, that it is not valid and binding, the declaration ends with the words, *k'dat Moshe v'Yisrael,* "in accordance with the tradition of the Jews," referred to in shorthand by invoking "Moses and Israel." Pretty powerful statements!

While this is the traditional formula, these are not the only words that you can use. (For some alternatives, see Appendix V.) Some liberal clergy will only use this formula, but many are open to at least some variations, and some are particularly creative and innovative. The words you choose can link you to age-old traditions, or they can intentionally distance you from aspects of the tradition with which you are not particularly comfortable or to which you cannot easily relate. They can be in Hebrew, or English, or both. You have the opportunity to consider what you want to say, and how you want to say it. Be sure to discuss your desires and concerns with your clergy.

As you plan your vows, consider also the people you will be inviting to your *kiddushin* and the message you want to convey to them. Your reciting the traditional vows may confer a degree of Jewish authenticity to a ceremony whose standing might be questionable for others. Your reciting any words in Hebrew may serve the same purpose. Your preparing your own personal vows may create a memorable moment, highlighting aspects of your relationship never considered by your guests. Lastly, it may be important to you to consider the impact that your choices can have on your ceremony's acceptance by the broader Jewish community.

A final note: Maintaining a relationship requires love, support and encouragement from others. Some couples have chosen to involve their families and friends in their *kiddushin* by having them take their own collective vow to nurture and sustain the couple. For example, before or after you take your vows, the clergy can say:

> *You are all here today because you have a history with _____ and _____, a history of love and friendship. Your standing around this chuppah symbolizes your support for them. Maintaining a marriage is no simple feat, and it does not depend merely on the efforts of the couple themselves. I therefore ask each of you to take your own vow to them now:*

> *Do you promise to affirm the love and commitment _____ and _____ share, and to support and nurture them as they grow and become the family, the partners, of whom they dream today?*

In your discussion with your clergy, you can decide what you would like to have said.

The Wedding Address

At some time during the ceremony, the officiant will speak directly to the two of you for a few minutes. Some speak generally of the meaning and responsibilities of marriage, interspersing their remarks with personal comments, based on personal memories of you and/or on the discussions they have had with you during your pre-marital meetings. Some elaborate on the particular themes that dominated your pre-marital discussions. Others draw on themes and messages of nearby Jewish holidays or the weekly Torah portion. You can discuss with the clergy, in advance, the approach that she/he plans to take, to be sure that it is one with which you will be comfortable.

Seven Blessings / Sheva B'rachot

The earliest ritual for marriage (*nisuin*) consisted of the recitation of a series of blessings, and nothing more. These blessings were said not under the *chuppah*, but rather at a large feast. Since the fusion of the ceremonies in the Middle Ages, these blessings, known in Hebrew as the *Sheva B'rachot* (literally "Seven Blessings"), have been a part of the ceremony itself. Here again, as with the circling, Jewish mystics attribute special significance to the number seven, seeing it as representing completion, creation and wholeness.

The traditional *Sheva B'rachot* use metaphors readily understood by earlier generations of Jews; however language and imagery are often less than accessible _____ gible to modern, liberal Jews. Nonetheless, their overarching themes remain powerful today:

> the human capacity to express joy, embodied in the
> symbol of wine;
> the wonder of creation;
> the creative and procreative power of humanity;
> the extraordinary nature of being human, imbued with
> a capacity to strive toward the divine;
> the healing and restorative capacity of meaningful
> relationships for the people involved and for the
> whole world;
> the joy we experience when celebrating the loving
> commitment of two people for each other;
> and the joy that those two people find in each other.

Liberal clergy have demonstrated a willingness to alter both the Hebrew and the English liturgical texts in a variety of ways. For example, since its inception, the Reform Movement has given the clergy the option of excluding some or all of the blessings. It has also offered linguistic modifications for some of the more traditional phrases.

There are many ways to incorporate these themes into your ceremony. In the early 1970's, some liberal Jews began to involve family and friends in their ceremonies by having them recite one or more of the *Sheva B'rachot*, or a substitute for them,

. Hebrew or English. During the past few decades, couples have begun to invite friends and family to offer their own personal blessings as well. Some couples choose to have the traditional blessings, or a reworked version of them, chanted during their *kiddushin*, followed either by a modern interpretive rendition in English or by personal blessings offered by guests. Some couples choose to have the traditional blessings chanted at the ceremony and to have friends offer their own blessings at the meal that follows. Others choose not to use the traditional blessings at all, but instead, ask friends or family members to prepare personal blessings on a pre-assigned theme. And others have the clergy give a brief explanation of the custom of offering blessings and then invite the guests to think of the blessings they hope you will enjoy together as the blessings are chanted in Hebrew. This is a wonderful opportunity to involve friends and family and to underscore the heightened sense of being blessed that you are likely to feel on the day of your *kiddushin*.

As an extension of the original custom, in many Jewish communities the *Sheva B'rachot* were chanted at the wedding reception or wedding meal as well as at the ceremony itself. They traditionally followed the recitation of the *Birkat HaMazon*, the Blessing after Meals. In today's liberal *kiddushin* the choice to include any form of the *Sheva B'rachot* is yours. (Texts for the traditional *Sheva B'rachot* and various alternatives in Hebrew and English are in Appendix VI. A liberal text for *Birkat HaMazon* is in Appendix VII.)

Breaking a Glass

Of all the customs associated with Jewish weddings in contemporary America, that of the groom's shattering a glass is probably the best known. In some communities the groom

breaks the glass under his foot; in others, he breaks it by throwing it against a wall. The origins of this convention are unclear. Some anthropologists believe that this is a symbolic rupturing of the bride's hymen; others point to a practice, shared by many cultures, of breaking a glass or a plate upon agreeing to a contract, in order to chase away or deceive evil spirits. The most widely known traditional interpretation of this custom is that even amidst joy, we must remember and mourn the destruction of the Temple. (For more information about the destruction of the Temple and its impact on Jewish wedding practices, see "Mourning Periods" in Chapter Four.) In some Moroccan Jewish villages, the custom of breaking the glass is understood as a way of fulfilling the talmudic maxim, "A difficult beginning is a good sign."

We in the West associate this act with the end of the official wedding ritual; other non-Western Jewish communities have their own customs. For example, in numerous communities in Africa and Asia, when the bride arrives at the groom's house to receive the wedding blessings and to consummate the marriage, she is greeted by her mother-in-law-to-be. As she approaches the door, she is given honey, egg, a glass of milk and a variety of other foods symbolic of the goodness and fertility that should accompany her marriage. After tasting them, or making a mixture of some of them and applying them to the wall, she takes the glass, along with an egg or perhaps a pomegranate, and throws it against the side of the house. Once that is done, the blessings and festivities commence. In some Moroccan communities, following the blessing for wine, the rabbi hands the goblet to the bride, who drinks from it and then lets the glass slip to the floor. If it breaks, the guests cry "The bad has been taken, happiness is destined!" In still other communities, the rabbi takes the glass after the members of the couple sip from it, and breaks it between them.

Since the nineteenth century, liberal Jews have devised new explanations for this custom, which have no ties with psychosexual symbolism, the Temple or the legality of the ceremony's contract. One interpretation is that you must treat your relationship with special care, for like glass, it is strong enough to hold your love, yet fragile enough to break easily. Another way of understanding this custom is that since life is neither all joy nor all sorrow, you must remember sadness, even at times of joy. Yet another view says that each piece of shattered glass symbolizes a year of joy to come for the couple.

While for liberal Jews this custom is optional, most couples choose to include it because of its power as a recognizable symbol and a binding and authentic ritual. In recent decades, many couples have chosen to have both members of the couple break a glass (or glasses) simultaneously to end their ceremony. Your decision about this will again be a reflection of your commitments and values.

A cautionary note: Your choices about who breaks the glass, and about who performs other formerly gender-bound rituals, such as who arrives at the *chuppah* first, might cause some of your guests to make assumptions about the roles you each take in your relationship. Do you have roles? Do you care if guests draw (potentially erroneous) conclusions about your roles in your relationship from your ritual decisions?

Would you like the clergy to say something to acknowledge their possible reactions? Do you want to address this in your explanatory booklet (see Chapter Four)? Will it be better to leave it alone? These issues are particularly important for same-sex couples.

Practical considerations: You want breaking the glass(es) to be as easy as possible. Therefore, buy one(s) made of thin glass. To prevent glass from flying or penetrating the bottom of your shoes, wrap the glass(es) in a thick napkin or cloth. Also, if your glass(es) will have stems, wrap the cloth tightly around the stem and loosely around the cup itself; this will make it easier for you to locate the part of the glass(es) that will shatter with the least resistance.

The Pronouncement

Although not part of Jewish tradition, it has become customary in most North American congregations and localities for clergy to end the ceremony by "pronouncing" that the couple is legally married. The officiant makes this statement as the official representative of the state. Like the breaking of the glass, this custom is technically optional, but is so prevalent in our images of weddings that most couples feel their *kiddushin* is not complete without it. In liberal circles, in response to the sexist overtones of the phrase "man and wife," some couples choose to substitute other phrases, such as "husband and wife," "wed," "a family," "a couple," "loving companions," or just "married." Here again, discussing your preferences and options in advance with your clergy can help you clarify the messages you wish to affirm for yourselves and for all those present.

Additional Blessings

Liberal *kiddushin* often include additional blessings marking the specialness of the occasion. Some of them are discussed below.

Shehecheyanu

On all "first" occasions, such as at the beginning of a holiday, or to acknowledge a new experience, Jewish custom is to recite a blessing known as "*Shehecheyanu*." You may be familiar with this prayer:

בָּרוּךְ אַתָּה יְיָ, אֱלֹהֵינוּ מֶלֶךְ הָעוֹלָם, שֶׁהֶחֱיָנוּ וְקִיְּמָנוּ וְהִגִּיעָנוּ לַזְּמַן הַזֶּה.

Baruch atah Adonai, Eloheinu Melech ha-olam, shehecheyanu, v'kiy'manu, v'higi-anu lazman hazeh.

Blessed are You, Adonai our God, Ruler of the Universe, who has given us life, sustained us and enabled us to reach this (joyous) time.

Sometimes clergy sing or recite this blessing. Sometimes everyone is invited to join in, to acknowledge the communal nature of the blessing. The placement of this prayer can vary. It can be used as part of the welcome, to set the tone; it can be used to punctuate the special moment of exchanging rings and vows. If you decide to include this prayer, you can discuss your preferences with your clergy.

The Priestly Blessing / Birkat Kohanim

Originally, on Yom Kippur, the Day of Atonement, the holiest day of the Jewish year, the High Priest, the *Kohen*, offered a blessing for the people, called *Birkat Kohanim*, the Priestly Blessing.

יְבָרֶכְךָ יְיָ וְיִשְׁמְרֶךָ.
יָאֵר יְיָ פָּנָיו אֵלֶיךָ וִיחֻנֶּךָּ.
יִשָּׂא יְיָ פָּנָיו אֵלֶיךָ וְיָשֵׂם לְךָ שָׁלוֹם.

Y'varech'cha Adonai v'yishm'recha.
Ya'eir Adonai panav eilecha vichuneka.
Yisa Adonai panav eilecha v'yaseim l'cha shalom.

May God bless you and keep you. May God's countenance shine upon you and be gracious to you. May God's countenance turn toward you and grant you peace.

In many Reform congregations, the clergy end Shabbat services with this prayer, blessing the congregants with this three-fold blessing as they leave the sanctuary to reenter the world.

Some Reform clergy place this prayer toward the beginning of the wedding ceremony. Others end *kiddushin* with it, to wish the couple, as they begin this new stage of life, the blessings of protection, good fortune and peace. If you decide to place it toward the end, expect it to come immediately prior to the "pronouncement" and the breaking of the glass.

Some Pre-Ceremony Rituals

Fasting

For most liberal Jews, the only Jewish fast they observe is on Yom Kippur. However, this is not the only fast that Jewish tradition knows. In fact, traditional Jews fast at a number of prescribed times, including the day of their wedding. In Judaism, fasting is a means of helping individuals or communities focus on their own inner lives, by removing themselves from the daily timetable that often revolves around meals and their preparation. Fasts are a means to foster repentance—literally, rethinking. Just as the fast of Yom Kippur helps us purify our souls and review our behavior and attitudes over the prior year before fully being prepared to embark upon a new one, so a fast on the day of your *kiddushin* can help you prepare your souls and hearts before embarking on this new era in your lives together. Fasting is not a common part of many contemporary Americans' normal rhythms; however, you may find this traditional means of setting time aside prior to your *kiddushin* for an emotional and spiritual assessment to be an attractive and meaningful ritual. If you choose to do so, be sure to consider your own physical and emotional responses to hunger and plan accordingly. You would not want to become irritable or ill in the hours leading up to your *kiddushin*!

Veiling / B'deken

In many parts of the world, women wear veils as a sign of modesty. We, who trace our earliest roots to the Middle East, can find evidence of this custom among Jews well into the twen-

tieth century. Dowry lists of Jewish brides from Yemen to Marrakesh demonstrate that the most plentiful single item listed among the bride's clothing was her collection of veils. In such a veiled world, it is easy to imagine how a young groom might be tricked into marrying a woman other than his intended! The rabbis trace our customs about veiling and unveiling the bride to the biblical story of Jacob, who worked for seven years to be able to marry his beloved, Rachel, only to find that he had been married to Rachel's sister, Leah; he only discovered her true identity when he awoke the next morning and saw her unveiled face.

The need to make sure that the bride is, indeed, the one desired has found expression in customs related to veiling and unveiling. In some Jewish communities, particularly those of Central and Eastern European origin, the groom has the honor and responsibility of placing the veil over his bride's face, in a ceremony known in Yiddish as *b'deken*, from the verb "to cover." In other Jewish circles, the groom lifts the bride's veil and lowers it during the ceremony itself, to inspect the bride. Curiously, a Hebrew word, *badak*, meaning  "check," accurately describes the groom's action and is remarkably similar in sound to the Yiddish verb *b'deken*. Whether the groom "covers" or "checks" his bride, the symbolism is important in a traditional Jewish ceremony. Even today, many couples choose to retain the veiling of the bride by the groom as a ceremonial preparatory moment prior to the actual *kiddushin*. However, responding to other cultural influences, many contemporary Western Jews have a custom of keeping the members of the couple separate until they approach the *chuppah*. When this custom is practiced, the groom can be given the opportunity during the ceremony to lift the veil and "check" the woman to whom he is about to pledge his loving commitment.

Many liberal Jews today consider the act of a man's placing a veil over a woman, or a woman's wearing a veil, highly objectionable. They associate the veil with societies in which women are expected to be subservient, and thus do not wish to include this symbol of a non-egalitarian relationship. Other liberal Jews use a diaphanous veil that permits the bride to see and to be seen. For them, a white wedding gown, veil and all, merely contributes to the pageantry and otherworldly aesthetic. Certainly a veil is not a necessity; like many of the other customs discussed here, it is an option, with many meanings and possible variations for you to consider.

An innovative reinterpretation of this tradition may speak to your modern sensibilities. Dressing and undressing another individual is an extremely intimate act. On the day of your *kiddushin*, perhaps you would enjoy choosing one article of clothing to put on each other just before the ceremony begins. It can be a planned private moment amidst the mayhem that will likely surround you. You can gaze into each other's eyes and gently touch each other before you symbolically dress each other. Any article of clothing will do—a cummerbund, a piece of jewelry, gloves, shoes, veil, *kippah*, *tallit*, etc. Thus, you can put the finishing touch on each other's clothing, in lieu of the traditional unilateral *b'deken*.

Tisch

In many Eastern European Jewish communities, the wedding celebration began *before* the couple arrived at the *chuppah*. Men and women gathered separately to rejoice, respectively, with the groom and the bride. The men gathered around a table, in Yiddish a *tisch*; the groom, and sometimes others, offered a discourse—relevant words, known  in Yiddish as a *wort* and in Hebrew as a *davar*—to set a spiritual context for the upcoming nuptials. The discourse focused on Jewish themes, drawn from the week's Torah portion or another Jewish text. The groom demonstrated his erudition and others offered advice and congratulations through their words. Following the *tisch*, bride and groom were led separately to the *chuppah*, led by their singing and dancing guests. The women's gathering was more personal and celebratory.

In recent years, some liberal Jews have reclaimed this custom, finding themselves drawn to the notion of setting time aside, in the frenzy of the final moments, to articulate a religious and spiritual message for all of the day's rejoicing. For those predisposed toward more traditional Jewish study and attuned to the Jewish cycle of Torah readings and holidays, the words usually relate to specifically Jewish themes. Others choose to share poetry and/or prose to capture the spiritual meaning of the moment for them. In liberal circles, a *tisch* is entirely optional. If you choose to include one, you should decide whether you want it to be a single-gender or mixed event, how many of your guests you would like to have in attendance, how many you will invite to speak, and what parameters you will set with regard to length and content.

Time Alone After the Ceremony / *Yichud*

Traditionally, following the wedding blessings, the couple went off to consummate their marriage. According to rabbis of different generations, *chuppah* originally referred to the private room to which a newly married couple retired to eat and to have sexual relations, thus making their *kiddushin* legally binding. The customs of Jewish communities from Eastern Europe to Morocco to Kurdistan attest to the universality of the practice of sequestering the couple in this manner and then seeking

verification of the consummation immediately thereafter. (This is the basis for all the "bloody sheet" stories your grandparents or others may have told you!)

Such customs have never been practiced by Reform Jews. However, the notion of your having some quiet, private time together immediately following the ceremony is one you ought seriously to consider. After the intensity of the last days of preparation, the growing nervousness of the hours right before the ceremony and the ceremony itself, many couples have found it a welcome relief to be alone together for a few minutes to acknowledge privately their new status, to talk, to hold each other, even to have a few bites of food, before they reenter the revelry of the reception. There is something very powerful and spiritually uplifting about having a few moments alone with each other, as you begin your religiously sanctioned life together as spouses. If you choose to do so, be sure to inform the clergy, as well as family, friends, caterer, bandleader and photographer in advance, so they can plan accordingly. You may even consider having the clergy announce that you will be taking some time for *yichud*, so that people do not worry about your where-abouts or disturb you during this private moment.

Involving Friends and Relatives in the Ceremony

As you have seen, there are many opportunities for friends and family to participate in your *kiddushin*. They can carry in or hold your *chuppah* during the ceremony. They can carry your rings for you and hand them to you at the appropriate time. Musical friends or family members can play instruments or sing, prior to, during or after your ceremony. Still other friends and family can share pre-selected readings during your ceremony. Jeff and Emily chose different sets  of people to sign their civil and their religious documents. Amy and Bill involved 21 friends by having seven chant the traditional blessings at the *chuppah*, seven more offer translations, and seven others offer their own personal blessings for them. Brian and Alma had seven people light the candles that encircled them under their *chuppah*; each candle brought light into their lives and their celebration and was a memorable way to share their ceremony with friends and family.

As you ponder your options, consider the impact that involving others will have on the flow, tone, length and aesthetic of your ceremony. Be aware that asking someone to participate is a unique way of expressing your love and respect for them, but also be sure to consider how those you care for most will feel when asked to participate. For example, how comfortable or anxious will they be speaking or performing in public? How will the heightened emotions of the occasion affect their ability to participate? It is important for you to discuss your desires and plans with the clergy, so that the contributions of your friends and family can be fully integrated into the ceremony. If you select the texts or music, be sure to provide people with their copies well in advance, so that they can become familiar and comfortable with their parts. If you have asked them to select or create their own texts(s), suggest that they bring a copy with them—otherwise, in the excitement of the moment, they may not be able to express themselves as clearly as they would like. In terms of  logistics, think about how best to ensure that those with active roles will be heard by everyone. Should they be seated near the *chuppah?* Will a microphone be necessary? How will people know their cues? Taking care of these details in advance will enable you to relax and more fully enjoy your ceremony.

If this is a remarriage for one or both of you and either of you has children, explore possibilities for acknowledging or including them during the ceremony. Do you want to have the clergy offer a particular message to them or blessing for them? Do you want to mention your children in  your vows? Will they have roles at your ceremony—flower girls, ring bearers, *chuppah* holders, best man, etc.? If the *chuppah* is a symbol of your new home, will you want your children to stand under it with you? Along the edges? Nearby? Beyond its periphery? Do *they* have ideas about how they want to participate, and about what will make them most comfortable?

Chapter Four

A Holy Context: The Non-Ritual Elements

Creating A Holy Context

At the beginning of your *kiddushin* you will be two separate individuals. At the end of your ceremony, a few short minutes later, you will be members of a single, new family. Symbolically, both the ceremony and the celebration repeatedly highlight your new identity as a family—both the two of you and your assembled guests need to get used to your new status! No matter how long you have been together, no matter how long your families and friends have known you as a couple, you have never before affirmed, ritually and publicly, your commitment to each other and to your shared future. Whatever your relationship has been with the members of your beloved's family, you do not become *relatives* until the day of your *kiddushin*. All of you are going through a transition, and through your ceremony and reception this change will be formally acknowledged.

How ready are the people in your lives to recognize the meaning your relationship has for you and to celebrate your *kiddushin* with you? How will you and others acknowledge your change of status? What can you do during your ceremony and at your reception that will be understood and appreciated by your guests as joyously affirming your new status and your new status relationships with the other members of your extended families?

During your *kiddushin*, through your words and gestures, you will affirm your desire to be family for each other. While  the ceremony may speak of specific things you offer each other, the truth is, the only thing the two of you are truly offering to each other is yourselves. That is what you and your guests will be celebrating—each of you freely offering your whole being to the other. So, with that in mind, how can you navigate through the planning and not lose sight of this? How can you insure that the day of your *kiddushin* will express what you mean to each other and what you value in each other? In other words, how can you create a context for your *kiddushin* that is holy? Quite simply, you will make the entire day of your *kiddushin* holy by being fully present, by not losing yourselves or any part of who you are, by being fully engaged with each other and with what is happening around you. You may be wondering how anything else could be possible. But many couples experience an increasing sense that the day is taking on a life of its own as the planning progresses. The visions, expectations, tastes and preferences of their family members, the caterers, band leaders, photographers, and florists come to overshadow their own. Some couples even look back on their wedding day and recall feeling somewhat disconnected, even alienated; parts of the ceremony and/or reception did not even vaguely reflect their desires or values.

Surely, you do not want that to happen to you. So, how can you avoid it? Easily: by taking time in advance, before you talk about any details with family and friends, to reflect on and share with each other your hopes and expectations for the day. Give yourselves ample time to do this, for this is extremely important.

Since childhood, each of you has had your own unique perceptions of and associations to weddings. You have heard stories about them and perhaps even attended some. Through movies, television, newspapers, magazines and books you have developed ideas of how a wedding "should be." You have formed your own opinions about what makes weddings meaningful, wonderful, frustrating or disastrous. Think about this, recalling the ways you have imagined your wedding in the past. What did it look like? Where was it? How large or small was it? Who was present? How were you and your guests dressed? What did people eat? What did you all *do*?

When you imagine the day of your *kiddushin* today, what does it look like? How does your old image compare with your current image? What do they share? What is different? What can you imagine happening on the day of your *kiddushin* that would offend your sensibilities or would make you cringe because of the implicit values conveyed? What moods would you like to create and what would you like to avoid?

Are your ideas for the ceremony similar to your ideas for the reception? Or are they very different, in size and/or tone? Will the tenor of the day be formal or informal, or somewhere in between? Will the decor be lavish or simple? Do you want the same people present for your ceremony as you do for your reception? While we do not consider the two parts as separate entities, planning as if they are can often alleviate the stress of trying to harmonize very different desires and needs. Perhaps a small, intimate ceremony is appealing to you, followed by a party with hundreds of friends and relatives. Or perhaps you want as many people as possible to share this special day with you from start to finish.

Once each of you has a better sense of what you want, share with each other both your old and your new images and expectations. How do they compare? What did you find you have in common? What do you disagree about? Is there room for negotiation? Together, identify aspects of your ceremony or celebration that you can agree upon, as well as those that are negotiable or in need of further serious discussion.

Next, reflect, first individually and then together, on your relationships with your families of origin. When was the last time you let family members help you make a major decision? When was the last time they made a major decision *for* you? How did you feel? How do you feel about turning to them now? Discuss with each other how involved you want or expect your families to be in the planning and/or the financing of your *kiddushin*. Agree on a stance for yourselves as a couple, and on how you will implement it together. This way, you will be able to sit down and comfortably and clearly explain your desires and expectations to those whom you hope will help to make them a reality.

Perhaps you will decide that your highest value is maintaining family harmony, *sh'lom bayit* (literally, peace in the home). Be prepared! Planning your *kiddushin* can seriously challenge your sense of *sh'lom bayit* within your relationship. Throughout the planning process, try to remain especially attuned to each other's needs and

reactions; you are going to learn a lot about how each of you communicates, handles stress, deals with your own and each other's families, and addresses conflict with each other and with others. In addition, together you will need to address the issue of *sh'lom bayit* as it relates to your own and each other's families. Keep in mind that the ways you interact with your in-laws-to-be can be setting a pattern for that relationship that will extend for many years into the future and may prove extremely hard to break. You may decide, for example, that for the sake of *sh'lom bayit* you will honor one parent's preferences for a part of the ceremony or reception, even if it is not what you would have chosen for yourselves. You may even find that you derive pleasure from the process of working with and compromising with the members of your soon-to-be extended families.

Whatever hassles normally accompany wedding plans, expect them to be compounded if you are merging two pre-existing households with children. In addition to both of you and your families of origin, you will be dealing with the families you have created. Your children and/or ex-spouses are likely to express their ambivalences and resistances, both verbally and non-verbally. You will need to find ways to respond, individually and together, in ways that move your plans ahead without dismissing or discounting the feelings of the children (and, perhaps, ex-spouses) who will continue to be a part of your lives.

Planning With Intention/*Kavanah*

Judaism teaches us that we should fully commit our hearts and minds to every aspect of our lives. It teaches us to engage the world with *kavanah*, with intent and forethought, with our hearts, souls and minds. When decisions and actions are imbued with *kavanah* they become reflections of our values and our essences. Remember: No decision is too mundane or too lofty to be worthy of your attention, to be approached with *kavanah*.

You can help insure that every aspect of your planning is imbued with *kavanah* if you give yourselves enough time to make every decision with the care and focus it deserves. Planning a wedding usually takes many months. Try to avoid rushing your decisions, so you can limit the risk of having to make choices under pressure tha you might later regret. Expect everything—including making decisions about your ceremony, choosing a band or hall, selecting your clothing, and choosing rings or having them made—to take twice as long as you thought it would. And assume everything will cost twice as much as you expected! That way, if you find you have time to spare or have run under budget, you can count yourselves lucky. Better that than your participating in a ceremony that lacks personal meaning, or going into debt, or being married in rings you do not like or plan to keep because the ones you *really* wanted did not get there in time!

Generally, the first decisions you will need to make will be selecting a date, choosing clergy—a rabbi and/or cantor—determining how many guests you will have, and deciding on a location. These can be done in any order, depending on your priorities. Other decisions related to the overall celebration have to do with the size of your wedding party, the type of food, music and decor you want, the photographic/videographic style (if any) you plan to use and the style and formality of clothing you and your guests will wear. If you approach the ceremony and celebration with *kavanah*, you can make them a coherent and meaningful whole. The remainder of this chapter will focus on the non-ritual elements of your *kiddushin* that you ought to consider.

Engaging Clergy

A Modern Jewish Phenomenon

Is having clergy at a wedding necessary according to Jewish tradition? No.

Historically, a rabbi's task was to insure that the wedding was done according to the laws of the Jewish community. He had no specific ceremonial role. Rather, when, in front of two male Jewish witnesses, a Jewish man gave a Jewish woman a written marriage document and then a ring that he declared to be a sign of marriage, a legal Jewish wedding had occurred.

In Hebrew, the officiant is known as the *m'sadeir kiddushin* (if it is a man) or the *m'saderet kiddushin* (if it is a woman). Literally, this translates as *the arranger of the kiddushin.*

 Technically, this person is there to make sure the details are carried out appropriately. At a liberal *kiddushin*, the clergy will lead you through the ceremony and offer you blessings. Remember: The validity of your liberal *kiddushin* is determined by what the two of you say and do; the officiant merely contextualizes and affirms it.

In America, we live in a largely secular, Christian-influenced environment. Most of our cultural cues and notions about family, weddings, funerals, etc., have been shaped to some degree by this dominant culture. Having an officiant who says "By the power vested in me . . . I now pronounce you. . ." has become normative in the United States, but this is not a reflection of a specifically Jewish understanding of the marriage ritual.

Clergy in America not only serve a religious function at weddings, they also serve a civil function. In most states, rabbis and cantors are both recognized as official representatives of the Jewish community and can legally officate at weddings. Their civil function is to witness the union and to attest to the state authorities in writing that it is legal and binding, usually by submitting a signed marriage license.

Availability and Fees

It is important for you to get a commitment from the clergy you want well in advance of your wedding. The lives of clergy people tend to be quite heavily scheduled, with many obligations booked months and even years in advance. Offering a number of possible dates will increase the likelihood that the clergy of your choice will be available for *your kiddushin.*

Most congregational clergy do not receive special fees for officiating at their congregants' life-cycle ceremonies, including *kiddushin.* However, in most congregations, it is customary for congregants to acknowledge the clergy's services through a donation to the synagogue or to a special clergy discretionary fund. If you do not belong to the congregation of the clergy you want to hire, you should expect to pay a fee. Fees vary significantly around the country, so you should be sure to ask the clergy directly.

Choosing Clergy

Are you, as a couple, connected to any clergy? If so, having "your" clergy present at your ceremony will enrich the experience for everyone.

If, as a couple, there is no clergy with whom you have a personal or congregational connection, think of those with whom you or your families have had a prior relationship and consider the possibility of reconnecting with them. Your shared history could provide an added personal dimension to your *kiddushin*.

If you have no personal connections to clergy, or do not know any clergy in the area in which you will be getting married, your first step is to do some homework. Finding the right clergy for you is like finding a therapist, or a partner for an important personal project. Your first task, then, is locating some clergy. Think of weddings you have attended at which you felt the clergy's tone and message were ones that resonated with you. Speak to friends and relatives for recommendations. Perhaps friends or relatives can ask their clergy for a local referral for you. You can always call the clergy at a local Reform congregation. Another option is to contact the local branch of the Union of American Hebrew Congregations (you can find them in the phone book, or on the Internet at *www.uahc.org*) and get information about clergy in your immediate area (see Appendix VIII).

Your next task is to narrow down your options, finding clergy with whom you can work comfortably. If you are in an area where there are many members of the clergy, don't immediately assume that the first person with whom you can make an appointment has to be the one for your *kiddushin*. Consider making preliminary appointments with several. Prepare for each initial meeting with clear goals. Are you looking for someone who will just show up at your wedding and perform the ritual? Are you looking for someone who will take time to get to know you and let you get to know them? Are you looking for someone who is concerned about your perspectives and preferences regarding Jewish ritual and practice? Do you want to be part of a decision-making process that will lead to an individualized, personal ritual? Or would you rather have a fixed liturgy, determined by the clergy? When you contact potential officiants, be ready to share your answers to these questions, so that you can fully explore the compatibility of your desires and expectations with those of the clergy.

Each liberal clergy person approaches wedding ceremonies differently. If, after your initial phone contacts, there are a few clergy with whom you would like to meet, call and make preliminary appointments. Be direct: Let each one know that you are in the process of selecting clergy and have not yet made any decision; it is unfair to let the clergy member assume that you are ready to have him/her officiate. A first meeting does not commit you to subsequent meetings unless you are absolutely sure that you would like to have that clergy person officiate. Once you find the clergy with whom you would like to proceed, be sure to cancel all appointments with others. Ideally, through this process, you will find someone who can help you arrange the *kiddushin* that you want. If it is a good match, you will find that you remember and value not only the day of your *kiddushin*, but also the time you spent meeting together.

Consistent with a commitment to informed decision-making and personal choice, Reform clergy make their own decisions about officiating at same-sex ceremonies. Some see absolute parity between gay and straight marriage; they offer all Jewish couples similar ceremonies. Others are willing to officiate at same-sex ceremonies but are not comfortable calling them marriages, weddings, or *kiddushin*. The ceremonies they conduct for gay and lesbian couples will differ from those they perform for straight couples. Finally, there are some Reform and other liberal clergy who will not officiate at a ceremony affirm-

ing and celebrating the union of a gay or lesbian couple. If you are seeking an officiant for your same-sex ceremony, you will need to do some homework about the clergy in your area to learn about their willingness to help you create the kind of ceremony you want. (For the names of Reform clergy in your area who officiate at same-sex ceremonies, contact the Central Conference of American Rabbis, the

American Conference of Cantors, or the Union of American Hebrew Congregations. See Appendix VIII.)

Choosing A Date

There are a number of things to consider when choosing a date for your *kiddushin*. First, imagine the type of ceremony you would like. Will there be enough time to meet with the clergy you have chosen and to prepare properly for the ritual? Will there be enough time (6 months to a year) to take care of the non-ritual details? What other considerations are there?

Considering Your Personal Calendars

Is there a particular time of year you would like to have the ceremony? Or a date that you would like to set aside? Take a look at your calendars together. Flip through your entries between now and then. Are there assignments, projects, conferences that you know will dominate your attention and energy in the intervening months? Are there exams or deadlines that will not be negotiable? Consult your co-workers, bosses, school calendars, to check whether there are foreseeable activities during the three to four weeks prior to that date that will distract you from the final preparations or preclude your being able to go away on a honeymoon. Follow this process for each date you are considering; the more conflicts and stresses you can avoid through careful planning, the more you will be able to enjoy the time leading up to your *kiddushin*.

Considering the Jewish Calendar

THE DAY OF THE WEEK

There has never been a particular day of the week on which Jews married; only one day, the Sabbath, Shabbat, when

they did *not* marry. However, in different places and in different eras certain days of the week were popular or customary. Interestingly, given the legal nature of weddings, many communities scheduled weddings for the day before the rabbinic court, or *beit din,* sat; thus if either party felt the terms of the marriage contract had been breached, or that the marriage was contracted under false pretenses, they could immediately ask the court for an annulment. In these communities, this meant that weddings were held on Sundays and Wednesdays, since it was customary for the *beit din* to meet on Mondays and Thursdays. However, there are *ketubot* (Jewish marriage documents—see Chapter Three for more information about *ketubot*) that attest to the fact that Jews have married on every day of the week except Shabbat.

By custom, most Jewish weddings in North America are currently celebrated on Saturday evening or Sunday. Nevertheless, any day but Shabbat is really a possibility. Saturday night and Sunday have become conventional in recent decades because of the ease with which most guests can attend. However, you should not feel bound by this convention as you plan your *kiddushin*.

In addition to our forebears' legal concerns, they developed some interesting folk customs related to choosing a wedding day. Perhaps their folk wisdom will appeal to you and guide your selection. In many communities, Tuesday is considered particularly lucky. This is based on a reading of the story of creation in the Torah, in which Tuesday is the only day whose creation was described as "good" twice, not just once as all the other days. Therefore, many Jews adopted the custom of planning new ventures—marrying, changing jobs, moving to a new home—to benefit from the extra dose of "goodness" they would enjoy on a Tuesday. In medieval Spain, Jews had the custom of marrying on the evening of the New Moon, *Rosh Chodesh,* a day traditionally celebrated on the Jewish calendar. They believed that if you married at the New Moon, your love, like the moon, would grow over time. Some couples choose to marry on Saturday evening, accompanied by a Havdalah service (a ceremony separating Shabbat from the weekdays) to symbolically underscore the separation between their lives before and after their *kiddushin*. Be creative and choose a day that holds special meaning for you.

SHABBAT AND HOLIDAYS

For centuries, Jewish custom has prohibited marriages at specific dates and times during the Jewish year. Traditional Judaism prohibits all forms of work on certain days: Shabbat, the Jewish Sabbath; holy days; and the beginning and ending days of longer holidays. Therefore, since traditional weddings involve a monetary transaction and the signing of a legal contract, both considered forms of work, they are prohibited at those times.

Although Reform Judaism has long since abandoned the notion of *kiddushin* as a legal business transaction, most Reform clergy have nevertheless retained the custom of not celebrating *kiddushin* on these days. The clergy you select will offer his/her personal practice regarding this age-old custom. If you are having trouble  relating to this custom, perhaps the following non-legal explanation, first offered by a medieval rabbi, will be meaningful for you: Shabbat and holidays are times of heightened joy, as are weddings; so as not to diminish the joy of either, we should celebrate them separately.

In reality, if you do wish to schedule a daytime wedding on either Shabbat or the first day of a holiday, you will probably find it difficult, if not impossible, to locate clergy who will officiate. Moreover, friends or family members who are more traditionally observant will be unlikely to come. However, if you schedule your *kiddushin* on the second day of a holiday, you may have an easier time making arrangements with Reform clergy, since most Reform congregations do not observe the second day of festivals. (The same will probably not be true for more traditionally observant friends and relatives, who might be offended by your non-traditional choice.) To consult the Jewish calendar for the coming years, you can check the Internet (see Appendix VIII).

MOURNING PERIODS: PERSONAL AND COLLECTIVE

As a rule, Judaism has separated the sadness of mourning from the joy of weddings. Mourning is understood to be a process that decreases in intensity over the course of the first year after a death. Traditionally, attending a wedding ceremony is permitted after the first week of mourning, but attending a celebratory reception is prohibited for up to a year. If the individuals celebrating their *kiddushin* are themselves mourners, traditional Judaism advises against celebrating the *kiddushin*, legislating postponement until at least 30 days after a death, unless this will cause financial hardship.

While there is clear wisdom in these long-standing practices, Reform Judaism leaves such decisions to the individuals involved. There is no single rule or norm that is right for everyone. If, God forbid, you find yourselves in such a circumstance, consult family, friends or your clergy to find ways of giving yourselves ample opportunities to fully experience both the grief and pain of your loss and the excitement and joy of your *kiddushin*.

Most contemporary liberal American Jews are unfamiliar with the notion of extended collective mourning. No single event has caused all liberal Jews annually to refrain from normal daily patterns to express a collective sense of grief. Some of you, perhaps, have set a morning or evening aside to attend a Holocaust memorial service or a *Kristallnacht* commemoration. For a brief time you focused your mind and emotions on the unfathomable pain and loss suffered by the Jewish people and all of humanity during Hitler's Third Reich. However, while the images and stories may have haunted your waking or dreaming hours, you probably did not alter your daily routine, nor did you go into mourning yourself.

Generations of rabbis believed that in response to profound communal loss, Jews in perpetuity should observe annual periods of extended mourning. The rabbis reasoned that the destruction of the Temple in Jerusalem, the focal point of our ancestors' divine worship, was such a loss. Destroyed twice, first in 586 B.C.E., then rebuilt but destroyed again in 70 C.E., the Temple was never again rebuilt. (The Temple's sacrificial rites were suspended, giving rise to new forms of worship that became the foundation for contemporary Jewish prayer.) According to Jewish tradition, both Temples were destroyed on the same day of the year, Tishah B'Av (the 9th day of the month of Av). In response, the rabbis decreed it as a day of communal mourning, prohibiting eating and celebrations. The medieval rabbis expanded the period for observing these prohibitions, including up to three weeks prior to the 9th of Av, as a perpetual period of collective mourning. During that time, weddings were not allowed to be celebrated.

Medieval rabbis also felt that the Jewish people had suffered a collective loss when, according to legend, Akiba, a great second-century rabbi, and his disciples all died during a period of a few weeks in the springtime. To remember their deaths, the rabbis legislated against celebrating weddings for a seven-week period, from Pesach (the holiday of Passover, which may fall any time from late March to mid-April) until Shavuot (the holiday of Pentecost, which may fall any time from late May to mid-June, always 7 weeks after Pesach). This period coincided with the barley harvest in ancient Israel, known as the period of the *Omer*.

Mourning was suspended on only one day, the 33rd day of counting the *Omer* (known as Lag BaOmer); in traditional communities it remains the only day from Pesach to Shavuot on which Jews can celebrate weddings. It is interesting to note that the rabbis and disciples whose memories are honored during this period all lived and died during the Roman Empire, where weddings had long been prohibited during a seven-week period in the spring. Thus, even long ago, Jews found a specifically Jewish rationale for adopting the dominant culture's marriage practices.

Reform Judaism believes that mourning cannot be legislated. Moreover, from its beginning, the Reform Movement has understood the growth of Judaism as it developed over the centuries to be a direct positive outgrowth of the suspension of the Temple's sacrifices. Therefore, we do not impose blackout periods on *kiddushin* due to collective mourning. Many Reform rabbis and cantors officiate at weddings throughout the year.

However, if you are planning your *kiddushin* in the spring, between Pesach and Shavuot (sometime between late March and mid-June), or during the weeks prior to and including Tishah B'Av (sometime between mid-July and mid-August), you should be aware that these collective mourning periods are still observed by more traditionally observant Jews, as well as by some Reform Jews. (For Reform Jews this is a matter of personal choice and conviction.) Consult your clergy and those potential guests who might observe these customs to be sure they will be able to celebrate with you. Consider whether or not it is important for you to plan your *kiddushin* during a period that is universally accepted by Jews. (To access Jewish calendar information, see Appendix VIII.)

Considering Convenience

What other limiting factors might you need to consider as you choose a date: the individuals on your guest list; the availability of the clergy you wish to have officiate; the availability of the place, band or caterer you wish to use; the accessibility of your desired location in a given season; the inability of important individuals to attend on certain dates; and the likelihood that a particular weekend (long weekend or otherwise) would make it easier or more difficult for people to attend? You need to figure out your own hierarchy of importance for these elements as you narrow in on a date.

Choosing A Location

Locations are more than mere places and spaces. Every site you contemplate has its own ambience and will, therefore, help set a particular tone or mood for your wedding.

Generally, couples find it useful to think through some of the issues involved in choosing a location prior to speaking with their families about the details. Who will be responsible for making the arrangements for the ceremony and the reception? How much of the planning and detail work do you want to be doing yourselves? With what types of decisions would you rather not be involved? Who are the other people you trust to handle some of these details?

Will holding the ceremony in a specifically Jewish loca-

tion, such as at a synagogue, be important for either or both of you? Will holding the ceremony in another kind of place, one that has particular meaning for you as a couple, be important?

Will having both the ceremony and the reception in one place be necessary or preferable? If you are considering using two locales, will you be responsible for your guests' transportation or will you assume that they will take responsibility for their own? How difficult is the drive from one place to the other? How easy is parking at the location(s) you are considering? If your "perfect" place is a bit off the beaten track, how easily will your guests find it, and can you provide clear directions, with a map?

Who are your guests and how mobile are they? Does the site permit ease of access to all facilities, including the restrooms, for someone with physical limitations?

How comfortable will the seating be? If the space you are considering is used for many different functions, how good are the sight lines (important for your guests' comfort during the ceremony)? How flexible is the space? Will the management of the facility dictate to you how long your reception can be, based on their needs? (Imagine being told you have to leave just when the celebration is really getting going!) Does the place have specific caterers or catering requirements? Can it cater to *your* food requirements? Do you need to consider special food, either for everyone or for particular guests—kosher, vegetarian, vegan, prepared for individuals with specific food allergies, etc.? Does the place have specific bands or florists with whom they have standing contracts or to whom they usually send clients? Will they allow you to bring in your own caterers, bands, etc.? If you use the "house" service providers, will they accommodate your specific needs, desires and choices?

Will the time of year and the weather conditions influence the range of locales you are considering? Will there be ready and varied accommodations for those guests who prefer to stay overnight? You don't want to find yourselves in the position of booking the "perfect place" only to find that your choice has put an undue strain on cherished guests. Some couples have planned for guests to arrive early; others have even reserved rooms at an inn or hotel, so that they and their guests can enjoy a celebratory weekend together.

The Wedding Party

Your wedding party (the people actually participating in your ceremony) can be of any size and may be composed of anyone you choose. It can be just the two of you. It can be you, your parents, grandparents, siblings and a collection of close friends and relatives. It can be you and your closest friends. It can be any configuration that appeals to you. You can have as many bridesmaids and groomsmen as  you please, or even none at all. The possibilities are endless for what your procession might look like, who might participate in it, and what your roles in it might be. Create the choreography that is most reflective of your images for and the tone you wish to set at your wedding. (For further options and considerations, see "Arriving at the *Chuppah*" in Chapter Three.)

The Reception

Rejoicing and Recognition

Prior to the institution of a multifaceted marriage ceremony, the nuptial celebration consisted of a feast at which the couple was offered blessings. In essence, the feast was the forum at which the necessary blessings were said, and it was from the feast that the couple absented themselves to consummate the marriage. By the Middle Ages, the blessings that were the hallmark of the wedding feast were incorporated into the ceremony that preceded it; the blessings were now sung under the *chuppah*, the symbol of the home or room in which the marriage would be consummated.

Once the feast ceased being the place for concluding the marriage rite, what was the purpose of a communal gathering? Why do we continue to have public celebrations? Because Judaism teaches that our lives are not lived in a vacuum; the changes  in an individual's life have an impact upon the life of the broader community. At your *kiddushin*, your joy is cause for others to rejoice. This perspective is reflected in a number of traditions associated with the wedding feast. The ancient custom of offering Seven Blessings, the *Sheva B'rachot*, allows family, friends and community to share their joy with you and with each other, and express their hopes that your joy will continue into the future. Another custom, dating from sometime before the sixth century of the Common Era, has those in attendance dancing and singing for the bride at her wedding. By the sixteenth century "gladdening the bride and groom and dancing in front of them" gained the status of a commandment, a *mitzvah*, that every Jew should fulfill. You, the couple celebrating *kiddushin*, cannot offer yourselves blessings nor can you entertain yourselves—the community is essential. In more traditionally observant communities, family and friends still perform these *mitzvot*.

As you plan your own celebration, think of ways to incorporate these *mitzvot* into your reception. How would you like to have the people who care about you offer you their good wishes, hopes and blessings during the reception? How can they ensure your enjoyment on your wedding day? It might be through toasts or actual blessings (see

"Seven Blessings / *Sheva B'rachot*" in Chapter Three). It might be through special dances or songs or poetry or other performances. Eastern European Jewish communities had a long tradition of a professional wedding entertainer, the *badchan*, who danced and sang, offering comical and satirical songs to the bride and groom. For centuries in Italy and Amsterdam, Jewish wedding parties were not complete unless personally-penned poems and riddles, written by friends and relatives, were read to entertain the bride, the groom and their guests.

A wide variety of customs arose around dances at a wedding reception. Dances can symbolically convey powerful  information, without utilizing words. The new couple's first dance together following the ceremony reminds everyone of their newly affirmed status. The custom of having parents dance with their own children and then with their child's new spouse both highlights enduring bonds and publicly reinforces new ones.

In Jewish communities of Eastern Europe, the reception was a time to acknowledge the changed status of the parents as well as the children. If the wedding was for the last (traditionally, male) child of a family, a special moment at the reception focused on that child's parents. Garlands, a traditional sign of funerals as well as weddings, were placed upon the parents' heads, and they were lifted up on chairs. They were then danced around the room in a special dance known as a *mazinke tantz*. In this way, the whole community was reminded of the unique mixture of sadness and joy felt by the parents as their last child left home and they became "empty nesters." In recent decades, lifting the couple and/or their parents up on chairs at a reception (whether or not it is their "last child's wedding") has become commonplace as a celebratory gesture, and the original meaning has been lost. If you are the last child in your family to get married, you might consider including some sort of recognition of your parents' new status.

One last consideration: Colloquially, many Jews of Eastern European extraction expressed their desire to live into old age by saying, "I hope to live to dance at my grand-  children's weddings." In recognition of the joy of celebrating such a milestone, some Jewish communities include a special dance for grandparents, known as a *bubbe's tantz* (grandmother's dance, literally). And, should you have living great-grandparents . . .

Tzedakah: Sharing Your Good Fortune With Others

Tzedakah means making the world just and fair, even though it is most commonly translated as charity. It is a *mitzvah*, a commandment, to engage in acts of *tzedakah*. Jewish tradition teaches us that we should always remember those members of our community who are less fortunate than ourselves, particularly at significant moments in our lives. A wedding is customarily a time to fulfill this *mitzvah*, and there are numerous creative avenues available today for you to do so. Many couples earmark a percentage of what they plan to spend on their weddings to give to their favorite charities or programs for the disadvantaged. Some people give food left over from their reception to those who are hungry in their city or town. (You can check with local food pantries, shelters and soup kitchens in your area.) Jen and Linda gave the flowers to a hospital; Helaine and Craig gave theirs to a nursing home. Bob and Melinda placed a small box in the middle of each table during the reception and asked their guests to contribute something to the less fortunate, so that everyone had an opportunity to fulfill this *mitzvah*. The possibilities are endless, and the impact that this act of *tzedakah* will have on both givers and receivers is immeasurable. It is also a wonderful way for you, as a new Jewish family, to establish a habit of joint charitable giving.

Food, Music and Photographic Mementos

Making decisions about food, music and photographic mementos involves a lot more than choosing caterers, bands and photographers/videographers. You need to decide first how formal a gathering you wish to have. Yours may be a casual, at-home celebration, with a pot luck dinner, pre-

taped music or music played by friends, and candid shots taken throughout the day or evening. Or your celebration may be more formal, necessitating the assistance of various service providers. Caterers' roles range from preparing and serving the food that you have selected to planning the entire affair, determining the order, timing and length of each element of the reception. Band-leaders' roles vary from playing the music you select in "sets" that you choose to being emcees and party organizers, deciding whether and when to announce special dances, and organizing "activities" throughout the reception. Photographers' styles fall on a continuum from providing candid shots to setting up elaborate set pieces. Videographers' approaches range from taping the ceremony and highlights of the reception to continually taping throughout the day, catching you and your guests in both spontaneous and orchestrated interactions. Some involve couples in the decision about editing an abbreviated version, while others do not.

Only you know what you want and what will make you most comfortable. Figure out what kind of assistance you want from service providers. Think about your own priorities in terms

of where you want to invest your time and energy. Then speak with couples who have recently had celebrations, about their experiences with service providers. (If you are renting a public space, consult the manager for comments on other providers as well.) Get detailed descriptions of the service providers' work styles; then interview each candidate. Ask clear questions about the roles they usually take and the levels of interaction and intervention they prefer. It is better to begin by asking them about their preferences rather than telling them yours. That way, you reduce the risk of their telling you what they think will make the sale, depicting their approach as compatible with yours, when actually it is not. Your choices in these matters are yet another way your celebration will reflect your values to your friends and community.

You also don't want any surprises. For example, Karen and Jeff loved the photographs from Donna's and Beth's ceremony. In particular, they loved the close-ups of them under the *chuppah*. However, neither of them thought through what might have been involved in getting these pictures. Jeff felt that one of the most moving, spiritual moments of his life was interrupted by a photographer's leaning around the rabbi and setting off a bright flash, just as he placed the ring on Karen's finger. When speaking with Donna and Beth later on, Jeff and Karen learned that Donna and Beth remembered the photographer's having done the same thing, but they hadn't found it a distraction at all. Ask lots of questions and don't be afraid to express your preferences, so that you will end up hiring people who will add to the meaning and beauty of the day, rather than leave you feeling uncomfortable or embarrassed.

If you are planning a less formal affair, don't assume that there will be less planning to do. Recognize, instead, that there will be a different type of planning needed. There will still be many details to be worked out. If you choose to have friends and family make food, provide music, take photos or make videos, speak with them about what you want and then ask a friend or family member to coordinate everything. That way, you won't end up juggling all of the details yourselves.

Your selections of food and music can enhance the specifically Jewish flavor of your celebration. For example, the food can be kosher or kosher style. In addition, Jews of different geographic origins have foods that they associate with Jewish celebrations; for Ashkenazi Jews, these include chopped liver (Jewish paté!), knishes, herring, etc. Putting some of your families' regional favorites on the menu can add a special culinary dimension to the celebration. You can have Jewish music—*klezmer*, Israeli folk music or music of different Jewish communities—played during your ceremony and at your reception. (To get a special wedding CD or sheet music for Jewish weddings, you can contact Transcontinental Music, the Reform Movement's music publication house. See Appendix VIII.) If there is certain music you particularly want, make sure the band you select is willing to learn it. A band's assurance that they can play "Jewish" dance music can mean anything from their having a large and varied repertoire to their knowing one "Jewish" tune, such as *"Hava Nagila,"* which they play over and over. If you want Jewish music, be sure to ask for a sampling of their repertoire.

A final consideration about photographs and video tapes: In your discussions with the clergy, find out if she or he has any restrictions regarding the taking of pictures or videotaping during the actual ceremony. You do not want to hire clergy and photographers/videographers whose ideas are not compatible or are not supportive of your desires.

Cost

As you consider the cost of your reception, try to remember that your wedding day is but one day in your lives. Planning a day that is memorable is, of course, desirable. However, arranging an occasion that cuts deep into your savings or causes you to go into debt will affect your lives or the lives of your family members long after the wedding is over. Now is the time to think through the long-term ramifications of the reception that you plan or that others plan for you. In Lithuania, in 1637, the rabbis expressed their concern that wedding and circumcision banquets were getting out of hand. Their solution to the problem was to rule that:

> Inasmuch as people are spending too much money unnecessarily on festive meals [at marriages, circumcisions, etc.], every Jewish community and settlement which has a rabbi is expected to assemble its officers and rabbi and to consider the number of guests which it is suitable for every individual, in view of his wealth and the occasion, to invite to a festive meal. (Jacob Rader Marcus, *The Jew in the Medieval World*, 195)

Fear not! Our contemporary liberal communities are not going to issue such an injunction! However, moderation and the personal and spiritual meaning of this occasion can serve as limiting factors. Ultimately, it is up to you to consider the costs, financial and psychological, as you plan your reception.

Clothing

A number of years ago, Rachel arrived at one of our premarital counseling sessions absolutely beaming. She had just tried on her mother's wedding dress and had found that she would be able to wear it at her own wedding. In exquisite detail, she described the softly colored, mul-

tilayered cloth of which it was made and the way that it would wrap around her body. It took me a few moments to realize that she was describing a sari! Although her father gave her a German-Jewish last name, her mother's family had emigrated to the United States from a Jewish community in India. Her images of family weddings included women in saris and sandals. For her, these were the clothes that would make her Jewish wedding traditional, meaningful and bound to her family's earlier generations.

There are no long-standing universal Jewish laws regarding specific wedding attire. Rather, the clothes we have worn have reflected the cultural norms of the peoples among whom we have lived. "Traditional" merely refers to local custom. Jewish brides in India have traditionally worn softly colored saris; in Morocco, they have worn red fezzes, embroidered shirts and slippers, and dark skirts; in parts of Muslim Africa, they have worn a single cloth draped over the shoulders and held by chains, and adorned with scarves; in Yemen, a bride's elaborate headdress consists of veils and bright coins; and in European countries, Jewish brides most often wear a white gown and veil. Jewish grooms around the world have also worn greatly varied "tra-

ditional" wedding clothes. In parts of Muslim Africa, they wear red clothing and special slippers; in twentieth-century England, a day wedding called for the groom and his entourage to don morning coats and top hats; in traditionally observant communities of Central and Eastern European descent, a groom wears a kippah (yarmulke, or skullcap), a tallit (prayer shawl) and a kittel (a white robe that some adult Jews wear at major life transitions, including marriage and death). In medieval Europe, both Christian and Jewish brides and grooms dressed all in white, placed ashes on their foreheads and wore garlands on their heads to reinforce the perceived similarity between marking a marriage and a death: Each was a significant life change; Each meant a shift in self-perception and family organization. Interestingly, each was also marked by a ritual that lasted seven days. (See discussion on the meaning of the number seven in Jewish life on page 37.) In the West, in time, the white clothing was reinterpreted to represent the purity of bride and groom, and the ashes and garlands were dropped.

As you select your clothing, carefully consider the options available to you and the significance of each at this important life transition. Hopefully, like Rachel, you will find clothing that will add a special and meaningful dimension for you.

A Wedding Booklet

As you have seen, a Jewish wedding can have many elements that distinguish it from non-Jewish weddings. And your liberal Jewish wedding may include some things that even your Jewish guests have never before participated in or witnessed. From the *chuppah* to the *ketubah,* to the possible absence of "vows" as one hears them on TV and in movies, to blessings said or sung in Hebrew, to the breaking of the glass, Jews and non-Jews alike may be uncertain about the symbolism or meaning that your ritual choices have for the two of you.

In response to this reality, some couples ask the clergy to include brief explanations of each symbol, and translations for all Hebrew used during the ceremony. Others choose to prepare a booklet for their guests. Booklets can contain anything you want—a formal welcome to your guests, an explanation and history of Jewish weddings, explanations of the symbols you have chosen to include, transliterations and/or translations for the Hebrew used during the ceremony, and/or directions for when it is customary to stand or sit or say "Amen" or "*mazal tov.*" You know the backgrounds of your guests, and can decide what will work best for you.

Chapter Five

A Holy Process:
Personal and Spiritual Preparation

Setting Time Aside Before Your *Kiddushin*

More often than not, the dizzying whir of details that envelop wedding preparations in contemporary America is so focused on guests and receptions that little thought or energy is given to personal, spiritual and religious preparation. And yet this is a profoundly important personal, spiritual and religious occasion. How, then, will you adequately prepare yourselves for the day of your *kiddushin*? Deciding to celebrate your relationship is one thing; acknowledging the impact of committing your life and your future to another human being is something else. With your *kiddushin*, your lives and the lives of your families, your friends and your communities will be altered forever. How are you preparing yourselves and others for this reality?

Only you know how best to prepare yourselves, individually and as a couple, for this momentous occasion. Is it quiet, personal, private time that you need? Is it time apart from each other? Is it time alone together? Are there people with whom you would like to spend some special time—reflective or celebratory— prior to your *kiddushin*? Is some combination of these preferable for either or both of you? Take the time to consider all this and structure specific time for yourselves; otherwise, your personal, spiritual and emotional preparation is likely to be overlooked or given short shrift as your *kiddushin* approaches. Don't deprive yourselves of the opportunity to enjoy the spiritual nourishment this personal time can offer. Schedule it in; make it as high a priority as your other preparations.

Gaining Clarity About Your Relationship

All peoples on earth have developed customs and ceremonies to heighten awareness of the importance of significant life cycle shifts in their midst. Changes in identity (i.e., from single to married, from married to widowed, from childless to parent, etc.) affect everyone in the community, most particularly family members. Everyone is entering unknown territory; everyone is experiencing mixed emotions. As joyous as marriage is, the act of placing one's well-being in another's care is fraught with heightened anxiety and fear. There is trepidation about what life will be like after marriage and even about whether or not the marriage will actually take place. To symbolically acknowledge and assuage these concerns, societies have devised customs that both identify these inherent risks and dangers and safeguard against their coming to be.

Over the centuries, Jewish communties have developed a number of different rituals and customs to facilitate the relationship transitions that occur as part of *kiddushin*. These customs have varied from place to place and from era to era. None are *de rigueur*. Most have fallen by the wayside among modern Westernized Jews, rejected as outmoded, superstitious or sexist. However, many liberal Jewish couples have found that reconsidering some of these customs, contemplating their inherent wisdom and creatively adapting them to modern sensibilities have enriched their spiritual lives at this important time. The sections below will introduce you to some of these pre-marital customs, which can promote and deepen your understanding of the profound identity transformation that is at the heart of your *kiddushin*. Take plenty of time to consider and select from among the rich spiritual opportunities that our tradition has to offer.

T'nai-im

As you prepare for your married life together, you are planning to entrust your futures to each other. You are implicitly and explicitly affirming your willingness to care about and respond to each other's needs, hopes and expectations. Documentary evidence reveals our ancestors' awareness of the material expectations that accompanied the formation of a new family (much like contemporary pre-nuptial agreements) and their apparent lack of concern about the personal, spiritual and emotional expectations. In a document known as *t'nai-im* (literally, "conditions" in Hebrew), generations of Jews enumerated the conditions that had to be fulfilled prior to the celebration of *kiddushin*. Generally, this legally binding, witnessed document stipulated the date of the ceremony, the value and contents of

the dowry to be given, the types of gifts to be exchanged prior to the wedding, and the damages to be paid if the actual nuptials never took place. Among some American traditional Jewish communities, *t'nai-im* are still prepared; however, most use intentionally vague language to prevent major legal problems from ensuing should the "conditions," as stipulated, not be followed. In some communities, this concern is so intense that the final document avoids *any* specifics and instead merely says "as agreed upon" about each item.

As with the many customs which focused on marriage as a financial transaction, the Reform community dispensed with formal, traditional *t'nai-im* several generations ago. Today, though, some liberal Jews are recognizing that there is a fundamental wisdom embedded in this age-old custom: It obligated people to discuss, in detail, the assumptions and expectations they held about their future.

Today, your parents are no longer expected to articulate and agree to the conditions related to your *kiddushin*. Now, *you* are responsible for thinking about what you need and want and expect, before you get married. Take time to identify areas of interest or concern and set time aside for serious discussion with each other. Don't settle for broad general statements. It is in the details that your most profound commitments and expectations will be revealed. As you learn more about each other, your spiritual and emotional bonds can grow deeper and more meaningful. Every aspect of life, even the seemingly mundane or inconsequential, can add purpose and meaning to your existence; every aspect can have a spiritual dimension. Following are some issues for discussion.

DUAL CAREER COMPATIBILITY If you have both agreed that you will be a two-career family, have you anticipated or made any assumptions or promises about whose career moves will take precedence, should your paths conflict? How do you plan to negotiate? How will your current commitments change if or when you have children? How much is each of you willing to compromise?

FAMILY PLANNING COMPATIBILITY If you both have said you want children, have you discussed how many children you each want? Or how long you expect to wait before bringing children into your lives? Or what you will do if you are unable to have your own biological children? What are your expectations about childcare, including maternity/paternity leave? What arrangements are you considering for stepchildren? How do you expect to handle enduring relationships with ex-spouses, ex-in-laws or family members of a deceased spouse?

FINANCIAL COMPATIBILITY   Will you handle money as you have to this point (joint or separate bank accounts, investments, etc.)? What changes in money management, if any, will you make? Do you have similar approaches to investing, saving and spending money? If not, how will you handle your differences? Does one of you come into the relationship with debts or continuing obligations to support a family or a business venture? If so, do you have the same assumptions about your future individual or mutual commitments to them? Is one of you entering your marriage with significantly more money than the other? If so, how do you each feel about it and how do you plan to deal with it?

EMOTIONAL COMPATIBILITY   How comfortable are you with each other's modes of expression? Can you read and respond to each other's emotional needs in ways that are understood and experienced by the other as loving, supportive and respectful? Are you comfortable with your established patterns of spending free time and holidays, and do you discuss any concerns you may have with each other? Are you anticipating any changes in these patterns after you get married? What do you think might precipitate such changes?

RELIGIOUS AND PSYCHOLOGICAL COMPATIBILITY Do you have similar expectations about how you plan to seek religious and spiritual fulfillment as individuals and as a family? Do you share the same religion now? If so, are your practices similar? How do you handle differences now, and will that change if you have children? Do you have similar attitudes and expectations about the types of psychological or spiritual assistance you might be willing to seek in times of conflict or crisis?

Feel free to add other concerns to this list. It is not meant to be exhaustive; rather it is intended to be a catalyst for honest sharing and exploration. You may find it helpful to examine some or all of these issues with a neutral third party, such as clergy or a mental health professional. Either during your discussions or following them, you may want to jot down, as your *t'nai-im*, your mutually agreed upon conditions and expectations.

In some traditional communities the affirmation of the *t'nai-im* occurs immediately prior to the *kiddushin* itself. An alternative custom is to have a separate ceremony for ratifying the *t'nai-im*, as a sign of engagement. In traditional communities of Eastern European origin, following the signing, the two mothers break a plate to symbolize the irreparable nature of the sealed agreement and, according to folklore, to chase away demons that might interfere with the upcoming nuptials. (See also discussion of "Breaking a Glass" in Chapter Three.)

Imagine transforming an ordinary engagement party into a holy occasion by including an affirmation of your *t'nai-im*. If you make your *t'nai-im* the focus of such an occasion, consider sharing some or all of the contents with your guests. If you create a written document, you can choose to make some of it public, to be read and signed at the celebration, while reserving other parts for codicils to be witnessed and signed in private.

As for symbolically marking the binding nature of the document, think creatively. Having your mothers break plates together may not speak to your sensibilities, or be feasible for you to include. Explore meaningful possibilities with each other and with others whose opinions you value.

Getting or Making a Ketubah

Beginning in the late 1960's and early 1970's, some liberal Jews began to create their own *ketubot*, focusing on the spiritual and religious commitments they planned to make to each other at their *kiddushin*, rather than on the economic obligations contained in the traditional *ketubah*. When innovative, modern *ketubot* were first introduced, those wishing to use one as part of their *kiddushin* had to create their own texts and find calligraphers and/or artists to make them. Today, there are many different prepared liberal *ketubot* that you can find in Jewish bookstores and on the Internet (see Appendix IV). There are few pre-printed *ketubot* for same-sex couples; since Hebrew is a gender-based language, the text of even a liberal *ketubah* needs to be modified to indicate that the members of the couple are of the same sex.

However, a wonderful way to remind yourselves of the meaning you ascribe to your relationship and to your *kiddushin* is to create your own text.  Since this document marks a spiritual transition, rather than a legal transaction, it can include anything you like. Spend some time together articulating your thoughts and feelings about the following issues: What do you most value in each other and in your relationship? What does being married mean to you? What kind of support and nurturing do you hope to offer each other? What special talents or aspects of your personalities do you hope will flourish in your home? What emotional, spiritual, and religious tones do you hope your home will embody and convey to your friends and family? Many couples find it helpful to consult existing *ketubot* for ideas and wording.

If you decide to have a *ketubah*, be sure to begin looking for one or working on one well in advance of your *kiddushin*. Be sure you give yourselves and those who might help you ample time to make unhurried decisions and to complete the final document well before the day of your *kiddushin*. There are many things to consider given the varieties of liberal *ketubot* that exist. Liberal *ketubot* come in different languages: English, Hebrew, Aramaic or any combination. They can be simple printed documents or elaborately  designed works of art with expert calligraphy, or anything in between. Their design, form and content are meant to reflect the tastes and predilections of the individual couple. Involving artistic friends or relatives in the design and preparation can add an additional layer of meaning to your *ketubah*. You can also choose to hire professional calligraphers or artists. Desktop publishing offers yet another opportunity for you to prepare just the *ketubah* you want.

Traditional *ketubot* are written in Aramaic and contain information affirming that the *kiddushin* took place on a specific date, in a specific place, and for a specific couple. They identify the members of the couple by their English and their Hebrew names. Hebrew names do not include surnames; they identify people as the sons or daughters of their parents. The traditional form is _[first name(s)]_ *ben* (son of) / *bat* (daughter of) _[father's first name(s)]_; for example, *Joseph ben Avraham* or *Miriam bat Moshe Mendel*. However, in liberal Jewish circles it is customary for children to be identified by the names of both their parents—*Joseph ben Avraham v'Sarah* ("*v'*" means "and" in Hebrew). For your *ketubah* you will need to decide whether you want to be identified by both your English and Hebrew names, and whether your Hebrew name will identify you as the child of both (or all) of your parents.

Hebrew dates can be confusing because the Jewish calendar is a solar/lunar calendar, while the Gregorian calendar is not. For example, Passover is always the fifteenth of *Nisan* on the Jewish calendar, but it can fall any time from late March to late April on the Gregorian one. To determine the Jewish date of your *kiddushin*, you must consult a Jewish calendar for the year you plan to marry. Remember, the Jewish New Year, *Rosh Hashanah*, is celebrated in early fall, not on January 1. Also, bear in mind that Jews count days starting at sunset, not at the stroke of midnight. So be careful! If you consult a calendar that has both Hebrew and Gregorian dates on it, remember: Your daytime wedding will correspond to the Gregorian date; however, your nighttime wedding will correspond to the *next day's* Gregorian date. Consult your clergy to make sure the information will appear correctly on your *ketubah*.

Some couples prefer to prepare a *ketubah* that will remain a private document; they choose not to have the contents of their *ketubah* read aloud during the ceremony. Others choose to communicate their own thoughts, promises and hopes for their relationship in a more personal form—a letter, a poem, a song, a picture—and to share the contents of their *ketubah* in private and at a time of their own choosing. Another way to personalize your *ketubah* is to leave room on it for additions in the years to come.

Finally, your *ketubah* can be a document that holds special meaning for you as a couple well beyond the day of your *kiddushin*. Some couples hang their *ketubah* on a wall, as a piece of art and as a daily reminder of the hopes and aspirations they shared at the time of their *kiddushin*. Many couples make a habit of reading their *ketubah* aloud to each other each year as part of their anniversary celebration. Your *ketubah* can be a document that adds special meaning to the months prior to your ceremony (as you prepare it), to your time under the *chuppah* (as it is read), and to your lives in the years to come (as you pass it daily, review or recollect it).

Some Preparatory Customs

Will your communities and families prepare themselves in any way for your impending change of status? Will they set aside time to acknowledge how your becoming someone's spouse will affect them? Will they take the opportunity to consider the new types of responsibilities you are assuming?

Aufruf

An *aufruf* is one way Jewish communities have traditionally dealt with these questions. In our secular society, with its focus on individuals, we rarely pause to ask or answer such questions. Judaism, on the other hand, with its communal focus, has considered and responded to them. For centuries, most significant life changes were celebrated and marked within the community,

often in the synagogue. Traditional Judaism, with its male-centered orientation, emphasizes that every stage of an individual man's life has an impact on the life of the community as a whole. At birth, he is welcomed into the community of Jews through his circumcision. At thirteen, he is welcomed into the community of men who are responsible for reading Torah. And at his wedding, he is welcomed into the community of those responsible for bringing a new generation of Jews into being, to replenish the community. As each milestone approaches, the community expectantly awaits its arrival, for their collective existence is going to be altered. With an impending marriage, the community has a special ceremony that prepares them for the *kiddushin*: an *aufruf*, reminding them publicly of the man's imminent status change. In most Jewish communities of European descent, on the Sabbath prior to the *kiddushin*, in the synagogue, the groom-to-be is called up—*aufruf* in Yiddish, *aliyah* in Hebrew—to recite blessings before and after the reading of the Torah.

This simple act is charged with symbolic meaning: It provides the family with a moment to bask in the joy and honor of having a child approach marriage, and it reminds the whole community that their relationship with him is changing. He will be a bachelor only a few more days; then he will become a husband, a man with a family of his own. Interestingly, in many communities of non-European origin, the calling to Torah is not a preparatory ritual, but rather a means to acknowledge the status change, occurring on the Shabbat following the *kiddushin*.

Liberal Jewish communities, with our egalitarian orientation, see the milestones of both male and female Jewish lives as worthy of communal celebration, and as important in the lives of the individuals, their families and their communities. At birth, ceremonies exist to welcome both boys and girls into the community. At thirteen, both boys and girls are welcomed into the community of Torah readers. And at marriage, special ceremonies provide opportunities for familial and communal recognition and celebration. For many decades, it has been customary in liberal Jewish congregations for the couple to be called up during a Friday evening service prior to their *kiddushin* to be blessed by the clergy in front of the open ark. In addition, for many liberal Jews, having an *aufruf* is still a meaningful and important ceremony. In accordance with our egalitarian values, either or both members of the couple are called up for the honor of blessing the Torah. In this way, the community recognizes its changing relationship to the members of the couple and the couple's changing status within the community.

If you are unaffiliated, or if the idea of an *aufruf* or a blessing in a synagogue is not meaningful for you, consider creating a ritual of your own. What community *is* important to you? How and where can you do something within that community so that its members can acknowledge your upcoming *kiddushin* and rejoice with you? What can you do that will convey the message that you are taking on new responsibilities? What can you do publicly that will remind other people in your life that all of your relationships will soon change, when your status changes? What might you do following your *kiddushin* to further acknowledge this change?

Mikveh

How will you make your encounter with your beloved at your *kiddushin* different from all previous encounters? How can you symbolically begin your lives together with a renewed or deepened sense of freshness and purity?

From time immemorial, people have recognized water for its cleansing, purifying and restorative qualities. Cross-culturally, immersion in running water has been the medium for altering an individual's state of being, either literally or metaphorically. For Jews, the place of ritual immersion is known as a *mikveh*. A *mikveh* is a place of flowing water; it can be any place from a bathhouse to a river. In a traditional community, prior to *kiddushin*, both bride and groom, accompanied by witnesses, ritually immerse themselves. Without such immersion, the *kiddushin* is not considered ritually kosher. In some parts of the world, immersion immediately precedes the wedding ceremony; in other places, it happens a few days before. In some parts of the world, members of the wedding party accompany the couple—men with the groom and women with the bride—to the *mikveh*; in others, it is family members only. In some Eastern communities, the bride is accompanied by her mother- and sisters-in-law-to-be. What an interesting way to encourage bonding and a new level of intimacy!

The proximity of *mikveh* and *kiddushin* is intentional. Symbolically, *mikveh* marks the beginning of the nuptials. To go to *mikveh* and then not stand under the *chuppah* represents an interruption of a sacred process. To prevent such an interruption from occurring, communities have devised ways of making sure that bride and groom are accompanied from the moment they immerse until the moment of their wedding. For the bride, whose marriage is dependent upon her purity and virginity, even her sleeping hours are not to be spent alone; in some communities, a female family member or young child sleeps with her.

How will you know that you are entering into the final stage of preparation for you *kiddushin*? Will it be a bachelor party or bridal shower? Will it be a meal with family or friends or just with each other? Will it be marked by a trip to the *mikveh*? In some liberal Jewish circles, women are using the visit to the *mikveh* as a means of sharing a sacred moment with a small group of female friends and relatives. They are creating new rituals to accompany the immersion that build upon this ancient ritual and imbue it with meanings reflecting their modern sensibilities. Some women have written their own ceremonies, incorporating traditional text, contemporary writings, personal reflections and music. Others have a group discussion about change and relationships and ask a friend to lead it. The ceremonies either take place at the *mikveh* or at a home and can occur prior to or immediately following immersion. Those who have included *mikveh* have found beauty and spiritual renewal in this recast ancient ritual. Most liberal Jewish men have not yet reclaimed this ritual. You may want to start a new trend!

Henna

In the days and hours immediately prior to your *kiddushin*, how will your close friends and family members offer you support and good wishes? Will you have some personal, quiet time with them? Will creating an opportunity for them to share their wisdom and encouragement add an emotionally or spiritually meaningful dimension to your final preparations? Are you planning anything special to physically prepare yourself for your *kiddushin*? How can you refocus your nervous energy back onto the meaning of your *kiddushin*?

Over the centuries, Jewish communities have devised ways for close friends and relatives to have special time to express their joy, support and good wishes to the bride and groom. In Eastern communities, as the nuptials approached, parents, grandparents, siblings, in-laws-to-be and close friends came together, united by this common purpose. At separate male and female gatherings, they gave expression to their sentiments both physically and verbally. By applying henna, believed to have protective powers, to the hair and skin of the groom and bride respectively, they gave tangible form to their desires for safety and good luck to accompany the couple in their new life together. Throughout the long, slow process of applying the henna, they had hours to share stories and songs that conveyed their well-wishes and warnings. The honor of applying the henna was bestowed on different individuals, depending on communal customs. In parts of Muslim Africa, the groom's entourage was responsible for applying the henna to his hands or other parts of his body. In some Eastern communities, the women of the groom's family, in particular his mother, had the honor of applying the henna to the bride.

In addition to being a symbol of protection, the henna enhanced the beauty of the bride and groom. By decorating their bodies, friends and family members helped ensure that they looked their best on the day of their *kiddushin*. The time together helped everyone refocus their nervous energy from the last minute details of the arrangements to the shared joys and expectations for the couple. Can you imagine ways to achieve these goals for yourselves? It may involve scheduling extra time for the gym, or for a massage or a visit to a spa. Perhaps you will find pleasure in creating an opportunity for those closest to you to spend some private, focused time with you or your spouse-to-be. Your family and friends may appreciate having a chance, literally and symbolically, to express their joy to you, their support for you, and their good wishes for your future. Think creatively—this is largely uncharted territory in contemporary liberal communities!

Food and Music

How can sharing meals in a festive setting enhance your preparation for your wedding? How can you make the meal a sacred moment unto itself, and not have it become a mini-wedding? Can you identify ways to help your soon-to-be-in-laws affirm their relationships with each of you and express their good wishes for you both?

Communities the world over have created rituals involving the provision and sharing of food. Such rituals have always been filled with great emotional and spiritual significance. To offer another human being sustenance is to express welcome, care and concern. To break bread with someone is to show trust. Food serves these same purposes in Jewish rituals as well; eating is a hallmark of Jewish celebrations, and pre-nuptial gatherings are no exception.

Jewish communities have created many interesting and colorful ways to fete the bridal couple prior to their *kiddushin*. In parts of Muslim Africa, a Jewish groom-to-be leads a cow dressed as a bride—draped in white, with a veil and with make-up around its eyes—into the courtyard of the bride-to-be, and slaughters it to provide food for a pre-marital feast for the bride and her family and friends. In other communities, the groom's father slaughters an animal for the entire community to consume. In still other communities, following the *mikveh*, it is custom-ary for the bride to have women sing to her throughout the night. As they sing, the groom's family provides the bride and the singers with trays of food. When the food runs out, the bride's family refills the trays and sends them back to the groom's home so that he and his entourage can eat. In parts of Morocco, for the month prior to the  wedding the groom sends platters of food to the bride and her family once a week. In Western communities, it has become cus-tomary for the families of the couple to provide a festive meal for family and friends, most often with musical entertainment, at some point prior to the wedding.

In all likelihood friends, relatives and co-workers will plan celebratory gatherings prior to your *kiddushin*. Consider how your appreciation for them might be enhanced or transformed, if you recall the traditional meanings conveyed through a shared meal. Think of opportunities the two of you might arrange to share food with your respective families. Be aware of what your providing food for them, or accepting food from them, might mean to them. Perhaps adding such meals to your schedule will help strengthen bonds with your in-laws-to-be.

Remembering the Past

What would it mean to you to make time to remember where you have come from, and to affirm enduring bonds with your past, as you prepare to enter this next stage in your life? How can sharing your memories of deceased loved ones with your spouse-to-be strengthen your relationship? How can it make your spouse-to-be more fully a member of your family?

Prior to *kiddushin*, Jews traditionally visit the graves of family members; it helps people reconnect with the past even as they prepare to move into the future. Visiting the cemetery can have similar meaning for you. Additionally, during your cer-

emony, you may choose to acknowledge individuals who are not physically present, but who are present for you spiritually. Some couples choose to light candles, read parts of

letters, or have a few words said (by themselves, another family member or the clergy) about these people. If there are people you wish to remember during your *kiddushin*, think through your options and select the one that feels most appropriate to you. Remember: While you wish to recall your loved one, you do not want to create a situation in which mourning and loss overshadow the joy of your *kiddushin*.

Chapter Six

Interfaith Marriage Ceremonies

The Reform Movement's Stance

Since the earliest discussions among Reform rabbis about modifying the traditional wedding ceremony, there have been differences of opinion regarding officiation at intermarriages. Some clergy reasoned that with the recognition and acceptance of civil marriages and divorces by Reform Judaism, officiation at intermarriages should be acceptable. Others argued that the integrity of the ceremony—its symbols, prayers and pledges—was predicated on a specifically Jewish world view and meaning structure; for non-Jews to take a vow, make a pledge or participate in a specific religious rite that is devoid of personal religious significance or weight for them is to compromise the meaning and value of the vows, pledges, rites and customs themselves. (It would be akin to an American taking an oath in England that assumes allegiance to the king and an understanding and acceptance of all English laws and customs.) The enduring decision of the Reform rabbinate was to take a formal stance against officiating at intermarriages. However, given the Reform Movement's respect for personal decision-making and informed choice, each rabbi or cantor has the right to decide whether to do so.

A large percentage of Reform clergy do not officiate at interfaith marriages. However, some Reform clergy will officiate at any ceremony that involves at least one Jew. Some clergy will co-officiate with clergy of other faiths; others will not, but will officiate at interfaith ceremonies that meet certain criteria. For example, many of the latter will work only with couples who agree to conform to any of an array of expectations: studying Judaism together prior to the wedding; demonstrating that they have developed a healthy respect for each other's religious practices; making a commitment to raising children as Jews; making a commitment to go through conversion in the future. Some of these clergy members limit the liturgical and ritual options available to the couple—only some vow variants are acceptable, only certain blessings can be said, only the Jew can say or do certain things.

Your Shared History of Religious Decision-Making

Many interfaith couples are caught off-guard when they confront wedding decisions with a religious content. They react as if they have never before made any decisions related to their different religious upbringings or practices, whereas, in truth, they have probably made a whole host of religious decisions over the course of their relationship. Choosing to ignore the religious practices of your partner, deciding to accompany your partner to a religious festival or ritual, or opting to abstain from reciting certain prayers, all reflect religious decisions you may have already made. Some of your decisions were reached after careful thought and consideration; others were spontaneous. All, nonetheless, were decisions.

If you have spent time with each other's families for a holiday gathering, how did you understand your attendance? Were you there as an observer? Were you there as a learner? Were you there under duress? Were you there as an act of solidarity with your partner? How did others understand your presence and your level of participation? Did they respond in a welcoming manner? Were they reticent about inviting you to participate or about including you in certain aspects of their celebration? Were they attempting to instruct you about the meaning, particular or universal, of their practice? Were they hoping you would come to embrace the beauty and teachings of their religion?

The first time you spent a holiday with your partner's family, how did you respond? Were you surprised by any of your responses? Did you agree with your partner about what did or did not constitute a religious practice or custom? Were you able to share your reactions with your partner? Was your partner sensitive and responsive to your feelings? How did you negotiate your differences?

How do you understand your own personal and family observances? How have you explained or introduced them to your partner? Have you felt comfortable acknowledging specifically religious meaning and content in your life? Have you intentionally or inadvertently downplayed them?

Our reactions to similar situations can vary radically over time. The differences between you and your spouse's religious beliefs or practices may not have seemed very important when you first met, when your lives and futures were less interdependent. Now that you are planning a life together, now that they are becoming an enduring part of your life, are you still experiencing them the same way? Will having children change your perspective? Will being asked to host family holiday celebrations from your spouse's religious tradition be problematic or uncomfortable for you? Take time now to discuss your reactions and share your concerns and fears with each other, as openly as you are able. The learning and negotiating that you engage in now can set the tone for all

future interactions about the place of religion and religious decision-making in your lives. There is no single way to resolve these issues; however, putting them off is not a solution at all. Many couples have found it helpful to meet with clergy members of each of their faiths, to openly discuss their religions and religious ideas with the help of someone who is knowledgeable and skilled in counseling. Other couples have found it helpful to spend time with other interfaith couples who are at different stages of life, to learn from their experiences.

Religious Decision-Making and Your Wedding

Even if you consider yourselves thoroughly secular, you are likely to be surprised by the number of religious, ethnic and cultural decisions that will arise as you plan your wedding. Indeed, most interfaith couples are shocked to find how emotionally invested they are in customs they themselves do not view as religious, but that resonate as both specifically religious and foreign to someone from another background. For example, to someone raised in a High Church tradition, it may seem both natural and normative for the couple to kneel during their wedding ceremony. In fact, whether or not the ceremony takes place in a church, the very act of kneeling authenticates the ritual. To be married without kneeling in the process is inconceivable. Yet to the Jewish partner, kneeling during any ceremony is alien and experienced as a specifically Christian practice. Jews do not kneel when they worship; Christians do. Furthermore, incorporating kneeling into the ceremony will surely cause discomfort and distress to many of the practicing Jews who attend. Indeed, many of the practicing Christians might also find it awkward and uncomfortable. This is but one example; virtually every choice you make will have an element of this in it.

One way to confront this reality is to explore with each other the prayers, choreography, rituals, etc., that each of you associates with a wedding ceremony. Challenge yourselves to be open with each other about your feelings. Think hard about what you believe and value, what you expect from and associate with the rituals you are discussing. Explain to each other which customs you have always expected to include in your wedding, and which ones your families have always included. Challenge yourself to imagine forgoing some of them, and imagine how your partner feels doing the same. Learn with each other (perhaps with the help of clergy) about the meanings your different traditions ascribe to each ritual element. Can you find or put together some non-religiously charged rituals that can serve the same functions? What will it be like to participate in prayers or rituals that have no particular meaning for you? How will you feel knowing that your partner may be participating in your wedding with that same degree of distance or detachment? Imagine how your families will react to the use or omission of certain symbols. How will you feel if symbols from both your traditions are juxtaposed, such as making the sign of the cross and then intoning a prayer in Hebrew? How would your communities understand such a combined ceremony? How would they interpret your willingness to participate in rituals that are not your own?

Ensuring that you will participate in a ceremony that is right for you, a ceremony that conveys the power of your commitment to each other and your deeply held values, may not be an easy task. However, it is worth all the time and energy you give it.

Choosing an Officiant

When looking for someone to officiate, many interfaith couples consult friends, family members and local clergy for recommendations. You will find that many Reform clergy are happy to meet with you to help you explore possibilities for your ceremony and to discuss potential conflicts and concerns—religious practices and beliefs, family holiday celebrations, and child rearing questions. Fewer Reform clergy will be willing to officiate at your ceremony. When you call, be sure to let the clergy know that you are an interfaith couple. State whether or not you plan to have clergy members of different faiths co-officiate. You can save yourselves and the clergy time and potential discomfort by clarifying these issues prior to your first meeting. Clergy who do not officiate at interfaith ceremonies may be able to recommend others who do, or to refer you to an organization that can give you some guidance.

Do not be discouraged by all this. After working through the materials above, you may conclude that a civil official can provide you with your ideal ceremony. Many judges and Justices of the Peace are willing to incorporate any or all of the religious rituals or customs that you wish to have. You may find that this is the most comfortable option for you and your families. Don't limit yourselves; check out all the options.

Appendix I

The Ceremony Checklist

Following is a list of ritual options for your *kiddushin*. Items in **bold** represent core parts of the ceremony. Check those things you plan to include.

- [ ] *Chuppah*
- [ ] Procession form: _____
- [ ] Circling

- [ ] **Welcome**
  Hebrew blessings: [ ] chanted [ ] recited
  English translation: [ ] chanted [ ] recited
- [ ] English greetings
- [ ] Explantory information about ceremony

- [ ] **First cup of wine**
  Blessing in Hebrew: [ ] chanted [ ] recited
  Blessing in English: [ ] chanted [ ] recited
  Blessing of betrothal: [ ] traditional Hebrew
        [ ] egalitarian [ ] English translation

- [ ] *Ketubah*
  Written in: [ ] Aramaic [ ] Hebrew [ ] English
  Text: [ ] traditional [ ] modern pre-printed [ ] personalized
  Signing: [ ] before ceremony [ ] during ceremony
  Reading: [ ] before ceremony (when it is signed)
        [ ] during the ceremony

☐ **Vows**
Hebrew: ☐ traditional formula ☐ other _____
English: ☐ literal translation of Hebrew
☐ other _____

☐ **Rings or other tokens**

☐ **Vow for family and friends**

☐ **Wedding address**

☐ **Wedding blessings**
Seven blessings / *Sheva B'rachot:* ☐ traditional Hebrew
☐ modified Hebrew
Translation: ☐ literal ☐ interpretive
☐ Creative blessings prepared by _____
Blessings ☐ read ☐ chanted
Blessings offered by ☐ clergy ☐ friends ☐ family

☐ **Breaking a glass**

☐ **Pronouncement**

☐ **Additional blessings**

☐ *Shehecheyanu*
☐ As part of welcome ☐ toward conclusion
☐ Recited ☐ chanted
Offered by ☐ clergy ☐ friends ☐ family

☐ Priestly Blessing / *Birkat Kohanim*
☐ When during the service: _____
☐ Recited ☐ chanted

☐ **Additional readings or songs**
☐ Selections: _____
☐ Invited particpants: _____

Pre- and post-ceremony rituals

- [ ] *Aufruf*
- [ ] *Mikveh*
- [ ] Henna
- [ ] Visiting the Cemetery
- [ ] Fasting
- [ ] *Tisch*
- [ ] *B'deken*
- [ ] *Yichud*

Appendix II

Planning Timeline

1 year to 6 months (prior to your *kiddushin)*

- [ ] Determine the size of your wedding—how many guests you anticipate
- [ ] Select a date
- [ ] Determine the degree of formality you desire
- [ ] Determine your budget
- [ ] If you are of East European Jewish descent and are planning to have children, schedule appointments to be tested for Tay-Sachs and other Jewish genetic diseases.

If you are planning your wedding in "high season," you should concretize your arrangements at this time for:

- [ ] Clergy
- [ ] A location for your ceremony
- [ ] A location for your reception
- [ ] A caterer
- [ ] A photographer/videographer

6 months to 4 months

If your wedding will not be in "high season" you should concretize your plans at this time for:

- [ ] Clergy
- [ ] A location for your ceremony
- [ ] A location for your reception
- [ ] A caterer
- [ ] A photographer/videographer

No matter the size or season of your wedding, you should make decisions about and concretize your arrangements for:

KETUBAH / JEWISH WEDDING CONTRACT (if you will have one)
- [ ] Look at available designs and texts . . . or . . .
- [ ] Design and write your own; get a calligrapher or artist to prepare it (most calligraphers and artists request a minimum of 4 to 6 months)

RINGS OR OTHER TOKENS TO BE EXCHANGED
- [ ] Find the right rings or tokens
- [ ] Have them sized or altered, if they are wearable
- [ ] If they will be engraved, select the text and leave ample time for the engraving

CLOTHING
- [ ] Select and order clothing with time for alterations and fittings (particularly if the bride and bridesmaids will wear formal gowns and dresses)

INVITATIONS
- [ ] Pick a style
- [ ] Determine the text
- [ ] Decide who is sending the invitations and in whose names the invitations are being extended—yours or your parents'?

PERSONAL PREPARATION
- [ ] Schedule dates and times

3 months

INVITATIONS
- [ ] Finalize your guest list
- [ ] If you will have formal engraved invitations, order them
- [ ] Proofread invitation text (particularly engraved invitations) and ask a meticulous third person to review it as well
- [ ] Begin to address the outer envelopes, if they will not be printed

FLOWERS
☐ Make arrangements with a florist

GIFTS
☐ Decide if you will use a gift registry and select the items you would like
☐ Choose gifts for each other and/or for members of your wedding party, if you will be giving them

HONEYMOON PLANS
☐ Decide where you want to go, how soon after the ceremony you will leave, how long you will be away, and how much you will spend
☐ Apply for vacation time
☐ Make reservations

LEGAL MATTERS
☐ Make an appointment with your lawyer(s) to prepare or change: wills, titles, mortgages (consider joint ownership and other options), advance directives, living wills, powers of attorney, etc.

Note for same-sex couples: If you are a same-sex couple, your status change will not be recognized by civil authorities. Therefore, your ceremony will not result in your becoming "next of kin." You should discuss with your lawyer ways to protect the relationship you will be ritually affirming. If you do not have a lawyer who is familiar with same-sex couple issues, contact Lambda Legal Defense and Education Fund (www.lambda.org). If your wills, powers of attorney, advance directives, health care proxies, joint ownership documents, etc., are not properly prepared, you may find yourselves unable to inherit from each other, unable to visit each other during a medical emergency or unable to make important medical and financial decisions for each other.

☐ Changing your name(s)

If either or both of you will be changing your name(s), start notifying appropriate people and institutions:

- Social Security
- Department of Motor Vehicles
- Credit cards
- Banks
- Voter registration
- Brokers—insurance, investment

FINANCIAL MATTERS

☐ Contact finacial institutions if you will be making changes in your accounts

2 months

DEALING WITH THE CIVIL AUTHORITIES

☐ Get the following information from the city or town clerk where the ceremony will be held:

- When you must pick up your marriage license / domestic partnership documentation
- The city or town clerk's office hours
- The type of identification you must bring with you
- The need for blood tests

☐ Put a date in your calendars to go to the city or town clerk (be sure to get time off from work to go and take care of the above)

☐ Make doctors' appointments, if necessary

PRE-CEREMONY CELEBRATIONS

If you will be having parties or gatherings prior to the day of the ceremony:

☐ Send out invitations

☐ Book the facility or make necessary arrangements

If you will be having a t'nai-im celebration:

☐ Work out the details of the ceremonial piece
☐ Send out invitations
☐ Book the facility or make necessary arrangements

4 to 6 weeks

Invitations
☐ Send out invitations
☐ Keep a running list of responses
☐ Make arrangements for out-of-town guests

Pre-ceremony synagogue rituals
☐ If you will be having an *aufruf,* practice the blessings
☐ If there will be a blessing at a service, make arrangements and set a date with the clergy

Honeymoon plans
☐ Decide what you want to take with you

Other
☐ Make appointments for hair, make-up, etc.
☐ Select a person to take care of the logistics on the day of your wedding:
  • Flow of guests
  • Setup
  • Getting marriage license to the ceremony
  • Bringing pens for signing civil and Jewish documents
  • Getting rings or tokens to the ceremony
☐ Review plans with caterer—menus and schedule
☐ Review plans with musicians—make your musical selections and provide music for any special pieces you want
☐ Review plans with florist

Transportation
☐ Make arrangements for transportation to and from the ceremony and reception for yourselves, your families, and your wedding party

Two weeks

AUFRUF, IF THERE WILL BE ONE

☐ Invite people

☐ Invite others to participate and provide them with texts for their parts

NEWSPAPER ANNOUNCEMENT, IF THERE WILL BE ONE

☐ Send text to newspaper

Last week prior to your *kiddushin*

☐ Finalize details for food and drinks, final guest count

☐ Finalize details for flowers

☐ Finalize details for music

☐ Finalize details for transportation

☐ Map out the day of your wedding, leaving what seems to be too much time to:
  - Sleep, at least a little
  - Get dressed (including hair, make-up, jewelry, etc., if you wear them)
  - Get to the place of the ceremony
  - Take pictures
  - Meet with clergy
  - Sign *ketubah*, if it will be signed prior to the ceremony

HONEYMOON PLANS

☐ Confirm reservations, including transportation

☐ Pack, including tickets

MARRIAGE LICENSE / DOMESTIC PARTNERSHIP DOCUMENTATION

☐ Pick up from the city or town clerk

Prepare the things you will be taking with you on your wedding day:

- [ ] Clothes for the ceremony and reception
- [ ] Civil marriage license
- [ ] *Ketubah,* if you will have one
- [ ] Rings or other tokens
- [ ] Text of vows
- [ ] Gifts for members of wedding party
- [ ] Remuneration for clergy

If you will be leaving directly for your honeymoon:

- [ ] Take clothes to travel in
- [ ] Take your suitcases
- [ ] Don't forget tickets, money, passports, etc.

The day of your *kiddushin* . . . ENJOY YOURSELVES!!

Appendix III

Chuppot

Most synagogues have a *chuppah*. However, if you wish to personalize your *chuppah* or to use one other than the synagogue's, you can contact your local Judaica store or any of the following resources:

J. Levine Judaica
Web: www.levinejudaica.com
Phone: 212-695-6888
(One of the largest Judaica stores in the world)

The Artist's Wedding Studio
Corinne Soikin Strauss
E-mail: corinne@chuppah.com
Web: www.chuppah.com
(Willing to work with gay and lesbian couples)

Simcha Tova
Tova Rabinowitz
E-mail: tova@simchatovah.com
Web: www.simchatovah.com
Phone: 800-655-1968
(Willing to work with gay and lesbian couples)

Chuppahs-on-Hudson
Phone: 888-chuppah
(Makes *chuppot* out of wood/vines, etc.)

Efod Art Embroidery
Adina Gatt
E-mail: efodgatt@inter.net.il
Web: www.efodgatt.co.il
Fax: 972-4-982-8304
(Willing to work with gay and lesbian couples)

Jeanette Kuvin Oren & N. Amanda Ford
E-mail: jeanette@kuvinoren.com
Web: www.kuvinoren.com
Phone: 203-389-6077
Fax: 203-389-6078

Original Design Huppah
Margery Langner
Phone: 516-593-4767
Fax: 800-517-1965

Precious Heirlooms
Patric Lembo
E-mail: preciousheirlooms@juno.com
Web: www.preciousheirlooms.com
Phone: 973-226-2447
Fax: 973-226-3840

REEVA's 'ritings with ruach
Reeva Shaffer
E-mail: reevas@aol.com
Phone: 703-467-9700
Fax: 703-467-9600
(Willing to work with gay and lesbian couples)

Shizre Kodesh
Robert Kleiman
E-mail: shizre@netvision.net.il
Web: www.shizre-kodesh.co.il
Phone: 972-2-627-4293
Fax: 972-2-627-3102

Appendix IV

Ketubot

In addition to consulting your clergy and friends who have had *ketubot* made for them, you can consult the Internet. Currently, you can find artists and samples of *ketubot* at the following:

Ketubah, Ketubah
E-mail: info@ketubah.com; ketubah@idirect.com
Web: www.ketubah.com
Phone: 800-ketubah

Judaica Connection
Web: www.JudaicConnection.com
(A wide variety of texts and artists, including 17 choices —by 4 artists—of same-sex "commitment vows")

Micah Parker ArtWorks
Web: www.MicahParkerartworks.com
(Open to working with original texts)

Jewish Weddings Catalogue
Web: www.ketubahs.com

Nishima
E-mail: Samanna@ucla.edu
Web: www.nishima.com
(All individualized *ketubot;* willing to work with gay and lesbian couples)

Appendix V

Vow Variations

From Song of Songs (6:3)

"I am my beloved's and my beloved is mine."

Said about a man:

Ani l'dodi v'dodi li

אֲנִי לְדוֹדִי וְדוֹדִי לִי

Said about a woman:

Ani l'dodati v'dodati li

אֲנִי לְדוֹדָתִי וְדוֹדָתִי לִי

From Psalms (89:4)

"I shall establish a covenant with my chosen one."

Said about a man:

Karati b'rit livchiri

כָּרַתִּי בְּרִית לִבְחִירִי

Said about a woman:

Karati b'rit livchirati

כָּרַתִּי בְּרִית לִבְחִירָתִי

From Genesis (9:12)

"This is a token (sign) of the covenant."

Said by either a man or woman:

Zot ot b'rit

זֹאת אוֹת בְּרִית

From II Samuel (23:5)

"For he/she has made an everlasting covenant with me."

Said about a man:

Ki v'rit olam sam li

כִּי בְרִית עוֹלָם שָׂם לִי

Said about a woman:

Ki v'rit olam samah li

כִּי בְרִית עוֹלָם שָׂמָה לִי

From Song of Songs (5:16)

"This is my beloved and this is my friend."

Said about a man:

Zeh dodi v'zeh rei-i

זֶה דוֹדִי וְזֶה רֵעִי

Said about a woman:

Zot dodati v'zot rayati

זֹאת דוֹדָתִי וְזֹאת רַעְיָתִי

From the Book of Ruth (1:16)

"Wherever you go, I will go; wherever you lodge, I will lodge; your people will be my people, and your God my God."

Said to a woman:

כִּי אֶל־אֲשֶׁר תֵּלְכִי אֵלֵךְ וּבַאֲשֶׁר תָּלִינִי אָלִין עַמֵּךְ עַמִּי וֵאלֹהַיִךְ אֱלֹהָי.

Ki el asher teil'chi, eileich; uvaasher talini, alin; ameich ami; v'Eilohai-ich Elohai.

Said to a man:

כִּי אֶל־אֲשֶׁר תֵּלֵךְ אֵלֵךְ וּבַאֲשֶׁר תָּלִין אָלִין עַמְּךָ עַמִּי וֵאלֹהֶיךָ אֱלֹהָי.

Ki el asher teileich, eileich; uvaasher talin, alin; amcha ami, v'Eilohechah Elohai.

From the First Book of Samuel (18:1)

"And it came to pass . . . that the soul of Jonathan was knit with the soul of David, and Jonathan loved him as his own soul."

וַיְהִי. . . וְנֶפֶשׁ יְהוֹנָתָן נִקְשְׁרָה בְּנֶפֶשׁ דָּוִד וַיֶּאֱהָבוֹ יְהוֹנָתָן כְּנַפְשׁוֹ.

Vay'hi...v'nefesh Y'honatan niksharah b'nefesh David, v'ye-ehavu Y'honatan k'nafsho.

Rather than end your vows with these words:

". . . according to the religion/tradition/laws/customs of Moses and Israel."

K'dat Moshe v'Yisrael   כְּדַת מֹשֶׁה וְיִשְׂרָאֵל

You may want to choose from these variations:

l'fi m'soroteinu hak'doshot   לְפִי מְסוֹרוֹתֵינוּ הַקְּדוֹשׁוֹת
        ". . . according to our holy traditions."

l'fi ham'sorot hak'doshot   לְפִי הַמְּסוֹרוֹת הַקְּדוֹשׁוֹת
        ". . . according to the holy traditions."

lifnei Elohim v'ha-eidim ha-eileh   לִפְנֵי אֱלֹהִים וְהָעֵדִים הָאֵלֶּה
        ". . . before God and these witnesses."

lifnei ha-eidim ha-eileh   לִפְנֵי הָעֵדִים הָאֵלֶּה
        ". . . before these witnesses."

Appendix VI

Sheva B'rachot Variations

Based on the traditional Seven Blessings, each group of contemporary American Jews has developed an interpretive translation consistent with their beliefs and ideology. Note the marked contrasts.

Traditional Hebrew

בָּרוּךְ אַתָּה יְיָ, אֱלֹהֵינוּ מֶלֶךְ הָעוֹלָם, בּוֹרֵא פְּרִי הַגָּפֶן.

בָּרוּךְ אַתָּה יְיָ, אֱלֹהֵינוּ מֶלֶךְ הָעוֹלָם, שֶׁהַכֹּל בָּרָא לִכְבוֹדוֹ.

בָּרוּךְ אַתָּה יְיָ, אֱלֹהֵינוּ מֶלֶךְ הָעוֹלָם, יוֹצֵר הָאָדָם.

בָּרוּךְ אַתָּה יְיָ, אֱלֹהֵינוּ מֶלֶךְ הָעוֹלָם, אֲשֶׁר יָצַר אֶת הָאָדָם בְּצַלְמוֹ, בְּצֶלֶם דְּמוּת תַּבְנִיתוֹ, וְהִתְקִין לוֹ מִמֶּנּוּ בִּנְיָן עֲדֵי עַד. בָּרוּךְ אַתָּה יְיָ, יוֹצֵר הָאָדָם.

שׂוֹשׂ תָּשִׂישׂ וְתָגֵל הָעֲקָרָה, בְּקִבּוּץ בָּנֶיהָ לְתוֹכָהּ בְּשִׂמְחָה. בָּרוּךְ אַתָּה יְיָ, מְשַׂמֵּחַ צִיּוֹן בְּבָנֶיהָ.

שַׂמֵּחַ תְּשַׂמַּח רֵעִים הָאֲהוּבִים, כְּשַׂמֵּחֲךָ יְצִירְךָ בְּגַן עֵדֶן מִקֶּדֶם. בָּרוּךְ אַתָּה יְיָ, מְשַׂמֵּחַ חָתָן וְכַלָּה.

בָּרוּךְ אַתָּה יְיָ, אֱלֹהֵינוּ מֶלֶךְ הָעוֹלָם, אֲשֶׁר בָּרָא שָׂשׂוֹן וְשִׂמְחָה, חָתָן וְכַלָּה גִּילָה רִנָּה, דִּיצָה וְחֶדְוָה, אַהֲבָה וְאַחֲוָה, שָׁלוֹם וְרֵעוּת. מְהֵרָה יְיָ אֱלֹהֵינוּ יִשָּׁמַע בְּעָרֵי יְהוּדָה וּבְחוּצוֹת יְרוּשָׁלַיִם קוֹל שָׂשׂוֹן וְקוֹל שִׂמְחָה, קוֹל חָתָן וְקוֹל כַּלָּה, קוֹל מִצְהֲלוֹת חֲתָנִים מֵחֻפָּתָם וּנְעָרִים מִמִּשְׁתֵּה נְגִינָתָם. בָּרוּךְ אַתָּה יְיָ, מְשַׂמֵּחַ חָתָן עִם הַכַּלָּה.

Reform English

We praise You, Adonai our God, Ruler of the universe, Creator of the fruit of the vine.

We praise You, Adonai our God, Ruler of the universe, Creator of all things for Your glory.

We praise You, Adonai our God, Ruler of the universe, Creator of *humankind.*

We praise You, Adonai our God, Ruler of the universe, Creator of *man and woman.* We praise You, Adonai our God, Ruler of the universe, *who creates us to share with You in life's everlasting renewal.*

We praise You, Adonai our God, *who causes Zion to rejoice in her children's happy return.*

We praise You, Adonai our God, *who causes bride and groom to rejoice. May these loving companions rejoice as have Your creatures since the days of creation.*

We praise You, Adonai our God, Ruler of the universe, Creator of joy and gladness, bride and groom, love and kinship, peace and friendship. O God, may there always be heard in the cities of Israel and in the streets of Jerusalem: the sounds of joy and happiness, the voice of the groom and the voice of the bride, the shouts of young people celebrating, and the *songs of children at play.* We praise You, our God, who causes the bride and groom to rejoice together.

Conservative English

Praised are You, O Lord our God, King of the universe, Creator of the fruit of the vine.

Praised are You, O Lord our God, King of the universe, who created all things for Your glory.

Praised are You, O Lord our God, King of the universe, Creator of *man*.

Praised are You, O Lord our God, King of the universe, *who created man and woman in Your image, fashioning woman from man as his mate, that together they might perpetuate life. Praised are You, Creator of man.*

May Zion rejoice as her children are restored to her in joy. Praised are You, O Lord, who causes Zion to rejoice at her children's return.

Grant perfect joy to these loving companions, as You did to the first man and woman in the Garden of Eden. Praised are You, O Lord, who grants the joy of bride and groom.

Praised are You, O Lord our God, King of the universe, who created joy and gladness, bride and groom, mirth, song, delight and rejoicing, love and harmony, peace and companionship. O Lord our God, may there ever be heard in the cities of Judah and in the streets of Jerusalem voices of joy and gladness, voices of bride and groom, *the jubilant voices of those joined in marriage under the bridal canopy, the voices of young people feasting and singing.* Praised are You, O Lord, who causes the groom to rejoice with the bride.

Orthodox English

Praised be Thou, O Lord our God, King of the universe, who hast created the fruit of the vine.

Praised be Thou, O Lord our God, King of the universe, who hast created all things to Thy glory.

Praised be Thou, O Lord our God, King of the universe who hast created *man.*

Praised be Thou, O Lord our God, King of the universe, *who hast made man in Thine image, after Thy likeness, and out of his very self, Thou hast prepared unto him a perpetual fabric. Praised be Thou, O Lord, who has created man.*

May she who is childless [Zion] be exceedingly glad and rejoice when her children shall be reunited in her midst in joy. Praised be Thou, O Lord, who gladdenest Zion through [restoring] her children.

Mayest Thou gladden the beloved friends [the newly married couple], as Thou didst gladden Thy creature [Adam] in the Garden of Eden in time of yore. Praised be Thou, O Lord our God, who gladdenest the bridegroom and the bride.

Praised be Thou, O Lord our God, King of the universe, who hast created joy and gladness, bridegroom and bride, rejoicing, song, pleasure and delight, love and brotherhood, peace and fellowship. Soon may there be heard in the cities of Judah, and in the streets of Jerusalem, the voice of joy and gladness, the voice of bridegroom and the voice of the bride, the *jubilant voice of bridegrooms from their nuptial canopies,* and of youths from their feasts of song. Praised be Thou, O Lord, who gladdenest the bridegroom and the bride.

Creative Renderings

Below are some Hebrew and English options for the *Sheva B'rachot*, the Seven Blessings:

1.

Blessed are You, Eternal our God, Ruler of the universe, Who creates the fruit of the vine.

Blessed are You, Eternal our God, Ruler of the universe, Who created all things for Your glory.

Blessed are You, Eternal our God, Ruler of the universe, Creator of humankind.

Blessed are You, Eternal our God, Ruler of the universe, Who created humanity in Your image. Blessed are You, Eternal, Creator of humankind.

May lonely Zion rejoice as her children return to her in joy. Blessed are You, Eternal, Who causes Zion to rejoice in her children.

May these two, lovers and companions, rejoice as did Your first creatures in Eden so long ago. Blessed are You, Eternal our God, Who causes these loving companions to rejoice.

Blessed are You, Eternal, Ruler of the universe, Who created happiness and joy, exultation, song, pleasure, delight, love, harmony, peace, and companionship. Soon, Eternal our God, may there be heard in the cities of Judah and in the courtyards of Jerusalem the sound of happiness and the sound of joy, the sound of bridegroom and the sound of bride, the sound of lovers' jubilation from their *chuppah,* and of young people from their feasts of song. Blessed are You, Eternal, Who causes these loving companions to rejoice.

Rabbi Joan S. Friedman

If you're using Joan Friedman's English (above), you may want to substitute the following Hebrew forms:

Blessing 6 — for two women

שַׂמֵּחַ תְּשַׂמַּח רֵעוֹת הָאֲהוּבוֹת כְּשַׂמֵּחֲךָ יְצִירְךָ בְּגַן עֵדֶן מִקֶּדֶם.
בָּרוּךְ אַתָּה יְיָ, מְשַׂמֵּחַ רֵעוֹת אֲהוּבוֹת.

Blessing 6 — for two men or a man and a woman

שַׂמֵּחַ תְּשַׂמַּח רֵעִים הָאֲהוּבִים כְּשַׂמֵּחֲךָ יְצִירְךָ בְּגַן עֵדֶן מִקֶּדֶם.
בָּרוּךְ אַתָּה יְיָ, מְשַׂמֵּחַ רֵעִים אֲהוּבִים.

Blessing 7 — for two women

בָּרוּךְ אַתָּה יְיָ, אֱלֹהֵינוּ מֶלֶךְ הָעוֹלָם, אֲשֶׁר בָּרָא שָׂשׂוֹן וְשִׂמְחָה, חָתָן
וְכַלָּה גִּילָה רִנָּה, דִּיצָה וְחֶדְוָה, אַהֲבָה וְאַחֲוָה, שָׁלוֹם וְרֵעוּת. מְהֵרָה יְיָ
אֱלֹהֵינוּ יִשָּׁמַע בְּעָרֵי יְהוּדָה וּבְחוּצוֹת יְרוּשָׁלַיִם קוֹל שָׂשׂוֹן וְקוֹל שִׂמְחָה,
קוֹל חָתָן וְקוֹל כַּלָּה, קוֹל מִצְהֲלוֹת רֵעוֹת מֵחֻפָּתָן וּנְעָרוֹת מִמִּשְׁתֵּה
נְגִינָתָן. בָּרוּךְ אַתָּה יְיָ, מְשַׂמֵּחַ רֵעוֹת אֲהוּבוֹת.

Blessing 7 — for two men or a man and a woman

בָּרוּךְ אַתָּה יְיָ, אֱלֹהֵינוּ מֶלֶךְ הָעוֹלָם, אֲשֶׁר בָּרָא שָׂשׂוֹן וְשִׂמְחָה, חָתָן
וְכַלָּה גִּילָה רִנָּה, דִּיצָה וְחֶדְוָה, אַהֲבָה וְאַחֲוָה, שָׁלוֹם וְרֵעוּת. מְהֵרָה יְיָ
אֱלֹהֵינוּ יִשָּׁמַע בְּעָרֵי יְהוּדָה וּבְחוּצוֹת יְרוּשָׁלַיִם קוֹל שָׂשׂוֹן וְקוֹל שִׂמְחָה,
קוֹל חָתָן וְקוֹל כַּלָּה, קוֹל מִצְהֲלוֹת רֵעִים מֵחֻפָּתָם וּנְעָרִים מִמִּשְׁתֵּה
נְגִינָתָם. בָּרוּךְ אַתָּה יְיָ, מְשַׂמֵּחַ רֵעִים אֲהוּבִים.

2.

Praised are You, Adonai our God, who rules the universe, for creating everything in Your glory.

Praised are You, Adonai our God, who rules the universe, for creating the human being.

Praised are You, Adonai our God, who rules the universe, who has implanted in every human being divine qualities and who has provided every person with an equal.

Let Jerusalem rejoice with the sounds of those who bring hope and happiness. Blessed are You, Adonai, for bringing joy to this couple.

Praised are You, Adonai, for creating happiness and joy, celebration and humor, pleasure and delight, love and respect, peace and friendship.

Adonai, our God, carry the jubilant voices of this celebration throughout our communities; may it echo in every *chuppah* and at every wedding feast. Praised are You, Adonai, for uniting this couple in sacred love.

Praised are You, Adonai our God, ruler of the universe, who created the fruit of the vine, our symbol of joy.

Rabbi Lester Polonsky

3.

We acknowledge God as the Unity of all things, expressing our appreciation for this wine, symbol and aid of our rejoicing.

We acknowledge God as the Unity of all things, realizing that each separate moment and every distinct object points to and shares in this oneness.

We acknowledge the Unity of all things, recognizing and appreciating the blessing of being human.

We acknowledge God as the Unity of all things, realizing the special gift of awareness that permits us to perceive this unity and the wonder we experience as a loving couple joined to live together.

May rejoicing resound throughout the world as the homeless are given homes, persecution and oppression cease, and all people learn to live in peace with each other and in harmony with nature.

We ask for abundance of love to surround this couple. May they be for each other lovers and friends, and may their love partake of the same innocence, purity, and sense of discovery that we imagine the first couple to have experienced.

We acknowledge God as the Unity of all things, and today we highlight joy and gladness, lovers, delight and cheer, love and harmony, peace and companionship. May we all witness the day when the dominant sounds throughout the world will be the sound of happiness, the voices of lovers, the sound of feasting and singing.

Praised is love; blessed be this union. May this loving couple rejoice together.

Rabbi Denise Eger

4.

We look to our ancestors for guidance and ask God's blessings:

Praised are You, Adonai, Ruler of the Universe, who creates the fruit of the vine.

Just as Sarah brought new life into this world, may God bless us with the ability to create a new life together—a life full of joy and laughter and happiness.

Just as Rebekah, at the well, satisfied Eliezer's thirst, may God bless us with the flow of generosity and loving kindness that permeates our home.

Rachel and Leah, as sisters, were the same yet different. May God bless us with the gift of respecting each other's capabilities and help each other grow in strength.

Just as Miriam helped lead her people to freedom, may God bless us with the power to inspire others to sing and dance freely.

Just as Deborah was a prophet and a judge, may God bless us with eyes to see the good and bad in this world so that we may be partners with God in *tikkun olam* (repairing the world).

And Ruth, who in love and devotion declared, "For wherever you go, I will go. Wherever you lodge, I will lodge; your people will be my people and your God shall be my God." May we be strengthened in our commitment to one another as we journey from year to year.

Rabbi Denise Eger

5.

As we celebrate with _____ and _____ on this wonderful occasion, we give thanks for the sweetness of their love and the sweetness in all nature.

We fully honor God when we live our lives with integrity and honesty. We rejoice in the courage and commitment that _____ and _____ express today and throughout their relationship.

"Just to be is a blessing; just to live is holy." Today we open ourselves to the beauty and wonder in all life.

All humanity was created in God's image. Today we are awakened to the preciousness of the Divine Spark within each of us and we marvel at the manifold beauty of each creation.

We dream of a time when all the people of Israel will celebrate loving, caring relationships such as this one. We will work for a time when the love of a woman for a woman or a man for a man will be cause for rejoicing among our people. May the day soon come when Israel will welcome *all* its people, when all refugees and exiles will be oppressed no longer.

We rejoice with _____ and _____ in complete joy, and we echo the tradition in thanksgiving for the creation of joy and gladness, pleasure and delight, love and harmony, peace and friendship. May the whole world soon join in wholehearted celebration and rejoicing in all loving relationships.

Rabbi Leila Gal Berner

6.

אַתְּ בְּרוּכָה יָהּ אֱלֹהֵינוּ חֵי הָעוֹלָמִים בּוֹרֵאת פְּרִי הַגָּפֶן.

אַתְּ בְּרוּכָה יָהּ אֱלֹהֵינוּ חֵי הָעוֹלָמִים שֶׁהַכֹּל נִבְרָא לִכְבוֹדָהּ.

אַתְּ בְּרוּכָה יָהּ אֱלֹהֵינוּ חֵי הָעוֹלָמִים יוֹצֶרֶת כָּל אֱנוֹשׁ.

אַתְּ בְּרוּכָה יָהּ אֱלֹהֵינוּ חֵי הָעוֹלָמִים יוֹצֶרֶת כָּל אֱנוֹשׁ בְּצֶלֶם דְּמוּת
תַּבְנִיתָהּ. אַתְּ בְּרוּכָה יָהּ יוֹצֶרֶת כָּל חַי.

אַתְּ בְּרוּכָה יָהּ מְשַׂמַּחַת צִיּוֹן בְּבָנֶיהָ וּבְנוֹתֶיהָ.

Blessing 6 (female)	אַתְּ בְּרוּכָה יָהּ מְשַׂמַּחַת רֵעוֹת אֲהוּבוֹת.
Blessing 6 (male or mixed)	אַתְּ בְּרוּכָה יָהּ מְשַׂמַּחַת רֵעִים אֲהוּבִים.

מְהֵרָה יָהּ אֱלֹהֵינוּ יִשָּׁמַע בְּעָרֵי יְהוּדָה וּבְחוּצוֹת יְרוּשָׁלַיִם קוֹל שָׂשׂוֹן
וְקוֹל שִׂמְחָה — גִּילָה רִנָּה, דִּיצָה וְחֶדְוָה, אַהֲבָה וְאַחֲוָה, שָׁלוֹם
וְרֵעוּת. אַתְּ בְּרוּכָה יָהּ מְשַׂמַּחַת . . .

Blessing 7 conclusion (female):	רֵעוֹת אֲהוּבוֹת.
Blessing 7 conclusion (male or mixed):	רֵעִים אֲהוּבִים.

You are blessed, O God, guardian of time and space, who creates the fruit of the vine.

We fully honor God when we live our lives with integrity and honesty. We rejoice in the courage and commitment that _____ and _____ express today and throughout their relationship.

We acknowledge God as the unity of all things, recognizing and appreciating the blessing of being human.

You are blessed, *Shechina*, guardian of time and space, who created humanity in Your image. You are blessed, Creator of life.

We dream of a time when all the people of Israel will celebrate loving, caring relationships such as this one. We will work for a time when the love of a woman for a woman or a man for a man will be cause for rejoicing among our people. May the day come when Israel will welcome *all* its people; when all refugees and exiles will be oppressed no longer.

We rejoice in the abundance of love which surrounds this couple. May _____ and _____ continue to be for each other lovers and friends.

Blessed is the creation of joy and celebration, lover and mate, gladness and jubilation, pleasure and delight, love and solidarity, friendship and peace. Soon may we hear the world rejoice and celebrate all loving relationships.

Rabbi Leila Gal Berner

7.

Blessed are You O God, for creating that wonder which is the world:
>The mountains, the oceans, the deserts,
>The forests and the fields
>—All is full of life.

Blessed are You O God, for the creation of all people.

Blessed are You O God, for creating all people in Your image.
>Each person reflects the wonder of creation.
>All people are sacred, creators of life.

May the joyous hope of a better world
>Inspire all people to work together
>For justice and thus for peace,
>So that the homeless will have homes,
>The hungry will be fed,
>The persecuted and oppressed will be free,
>And all people will learn

To live in peace with each other
And in harmony with their environment.

We surround this couple with our love.
May they be for each other lovers and friends.
May their individual gifts help them
To create new worlds together.

Blessed are You O God, Creator of joy and gladness,
Song, laughter, good luck, hope,
Love, happiness,
Peace and friendship.
May we all witness the day
When the dominant sounds
In Jerusalem
And throughout the world
Will be these sounds of happiness:
The voices of lovers,
The sounds of feasting and singing,
And the songs of peace.
May these beloved companions rejoice together.

We give thanks to the Eternal Source of Creation
That gives us the fruit of the vine,
Symbol of our rejoicing.

Rabbi Stacy Offner

בָּרוּךְ אַתָּה יָהּ אֱלֹהֵינוּ מְקוֹר חַיִּים יוֹצֵר כָּל חַי.

בְּרוּכָה אַתְּ יָהּ נִשְׁמַת חַיִּים, בּוֹרֵאת כָּל נְשָׁמָה, אֲשֶׁר בַּיּוֹם הַשִּׁשִּׁי אָמְרָה, נַעֲשֶׂה חַיִּים בְּצַלְמֵנוּ כִּדְמוּתֵנוּ, זָכָר וּנְקֵבָה בָּרָאָה אוֹתָנוּ.

אֵימָתַי כִּי רַבִּים הָיוּ עִמָּדִי וּמִי הֵם אֵלוּ הַמַּלְאָכִים שֶׁהֵם מְשַׁמְּרִין אֶת הָאָדָם אָמַר ר' יְהוֹשֻׁעַ בֶּן לֵוִי אִיקוֹוֹנְיָה מְהַלֶּכֶת לִפְנֵי הָאָדָם וְהַכְּרוֹזוֹת כּוֹרְזִין לְפָנָיו וּמָה הֵן אוֹמְרִים תְּנוּ מָקוֹם לְאִיקוֹנִין שֶׁל הַקָּדוֹשׁ בָּרוּךְ הוּא. בָּרוּךְ אַתָּה הַקָּדוֹשׁ בָּרוּךְ הוּא בּוֹרֵא חַיִּים, מְשַׁנֶּה הַבְּרִיּוֹת.

שִׁיר הַמַּעֲלוֹת
בְּשׁוּב הָרוֹעָה אֶת שִׁיבַת צִיּוֹן הָיִינוּ כְּחוֹלְמִים אָז יִמָּלֵא שְׂחוֹק פִּינוּ וּלְשׁוֹנֵנוּ רִנָּה. בְּרוּכָה אַתְּ רוֹעַת יִשְׂרָאֵל מְקוֹר שְׂחוֹק וְרִנָּה.

שַׂמֵּחַ תְּשַׂמְּחִי רֵעוּת אֲהוּבוֹת כְּשֵׁם שֶׁשִּׂמַּחַתְּ בַּיּוֹם הַשִּׁשִּׁי לְמַעֲשֵׂה בְרִיאָתֵךְ כַּאֲשֶׁר רָאִית אֶת כָּל אֲשֶׁר עָשִׂית וְהִנֵּה־טוֹב מְאֹד. בְּרוּכָה אַתְּ יָהּ, בּוֹרֵאת שָׁמַיִם וָאָרֶץ, הַמְּלַמֶּדֶת אוֹתָנוּ גִּילָה וְשִׂמְחָה בְּמַעֲשֵׂי יָדֵינוּ.

בְּרוּכָה אַתְּ יָהּ אֱלֹהוּתֵנוּ מְקוֹר חַיִּים אֲשֶׁר בָּרְאָה שָׂשׂוֹן וְשִׂמְחָה, חֶבְרָה וּקְהִילָה, גִּילָה רִנָּה, דִּיצָה וְחֶדְוָה, אַהֲבָה וְאַחֲוָה, וְשָׁלוֹם וְרֵעוּת. מְהֵרָה יָהּ אֱלֹהוּתֵנוּ יִשָּׁמַע בָּעוֹלָם הַזֶּה, קוֹל שָׂשׂוֹן וְקוֹל שִׂמְחָה, קוֹל יְדִידָה וְקוֹל אֲהוּבָה, קוֹל מִצְהָלוֹת אֲהוּבוֹת מֵחוּפָּתָן, וְשִׁירֵי שָׁלוֹם מִמִּשְׁתֵּה נְגִינָתָן. בְּרוּכָה אַתְּ יָהּ, הַמְּאַחֶדֶת יְחִידוֹת בְּאַהֲבָה.

וּשְׁאַבְתֶּן מַיִם בְּשָׂשׂוֹן מִמַּעַיְנֵי הַיְשׁוּעָה בְּרוּכָה אַתְּ יָהּ מְקוֹר מַיִם־חַיִּים הַמְּקָרֶבֶת אֲהוּבוֹת כְּמַעְיָן גַּנִּים לִבְאֵר מַיִם חַיִּים.

Blessed are You, Yah, our God, Source of Life, who created all life.

Blessed are You, Yah, Breath of life, creator of every living soul, who on the sixth day said: Let us make life in our image, after our likeness, male and female you created us.

Says the Psalmist: 'There are many with me.' [Ps. 55:19] And who are they? They are the angels who watch our people. Rabbi Yehoshua ben Levi said: An entourage of angels always walks in front of people, with messengers calling out. What do they say? 'Make way for the image of the Holy Blessed One.' Blessed are You, Holy One of Blessing, Creator of life, who varies the forms of creation.

When the Shepherdess returned us to Zion, we were like dreamers. Then our mouths filled with laughter and our tongues with joy. Blessed are You, Protector of Israel, source of laughter and joy.

Bestow happiness on these loving companions, the same joy You felt on the sixth day of Your creation, when You saw all You had created and 'behold, it was *tov me'od.*' Blessed are You, Yah, Creator of heaven and earth, who teaches us to rejoice and be glad in the work of our hands.

Blessed are You, Yah, Source of Life, who created joy and celebration, friendship and community, gladness and song, gaiety and delight, love and harmony, peace and companionship. Soon may we hear in this world the voices of the lover, the joyous shouts of lovers from their canopy, and songs of peace from their music filled feasts. Blessed are You, Yah, who unites individuals through love.

Draw water in joy from the wells of liberation. Blessed are You, Yah, Fountain of living waters, who draws lovers to each other as a garden spring to a well of living waters.

Rabbi Lisa Edwards and Tracy Moore

❖

Alternate wordings for *Sheva B'rachot*

Below are some Hebrew variants either for same-sex ceremonies or for any couple wishing to remove gender- or role-specific language. Many of them can be inserted without changing the meter of the blessings, so that they can be sung to standard tunes:

1.

chatanim — חֲתָנִים — grooms
is changed to

"friends/companions"

rei-im (male or mixed)	רֵעִים
rei-ot (female)	רֵעוֹת

or "lovers"

ahuvim (male or mixed)	אֲהוּבִים
ahuvot (female)	אֲהוּבוֹת

2.

chatan im hakallah / חָתָן עִם הַכַּלָּה / groom with the bride
is changed to "loving companions":

rei-im haahuvim (male or mixed)	רֵעִים הָאֲהוּבִים
rei-ot haahuvot (female)	רֵעוֹת הָאֲהוּבוֹת

3.

m'samei-ach chatan im hakallah / מְשַׂמֵּחַ חָתָן עִם הַכַּלָּה
"who causes groom and bride to rejoice"
is changed to "who unites individuals in love":

Male or mixed

ham'acheid y'chidim b'ahavah	הַמְאַחֵד יְחִידִים בְּאַהֲבָה.

Female

ham'achedet y'chidot b'ahavah   הַמְּאַחֶדֶת יְחִידוֹת בְּאַהֲבָה.

4.

kol chatan v'kol kallah / קוֹל חָתָן וְקוֹל כַּלָּה
"voice of the groom and voice of the bride" is changed to

"the voice of honor and the voice of strength/courage"
(Not gender-specific):

kol kavod v'kol gevurah   קוֹל כָּבוֹד וְקוֹל גְּבוּרָה

or "the voice of lovers"

kol y'did v'kol ahuv (two men)   קוֹל יְדִיד וְקוֹל אָהוּב

kol y'didah v'kol ahuvah (two women)   קוֹל יְדִידָה וְקוֹל אֲהוּבָה

kol y'did v'kol ahuvah (male and female)   קוֹל יְדִיד וְקוֹל אֲהוּבָה

kol y'didah v'kol ahuv (female and male)   קוֹל יְדִידָה וְקוֹל אָהוּב

5.

chatan v'kallah / חָתָן וְכַלָּה / groom and bride
is changed to:

"friends/companions and lovers"

rei-im v'ahuvim (male or mixed)   רֵעִים וַאֲהוּבִים

rei-ot v'ahuvot (female)   רֵעוֹת וַאֲהוּבוֹת

or "beloved and friend"

dod v'rei-a (two men)   דּוֹד וְרֵעַ

dodah v'rei-ah (two women)   דּוֹדָה וְרֵעָה

dod v'rei-ah (male and female)   דּוֹד וְרֵעָה

dodah v'rei-a (female and male)   דּוֹדָה וְרֵעַ

or "one who loves and one who is loved"

oheiv v'ahuv (two men)	אוֹהֵב וְאָהוּב
ohevet v'ahuvah (two women)	אוֹהֶבֶת וַאֲהוּבָה
oheiv v'ahuvah (male and female)	אוֹהֵב וַאֲהוּבָה
ohevet v'ahuv (female and male)	אוֹהֶבֶת וְאָהוּב

Appendix VII

Birkat Hamazon
Blessing after Meal for Weddings

Some people choose to do a formal Hebrew and/or English Grace After Meals, followed by the Sheva B'rachot.

ALL:

Shir Hamaalot b'shuv Adonai	שִׁיר הַמַּעֲלוֹת בְּשׁוּב יְיָ
et shivat Tziyon,	אֶת־שִׁיבַת־צִיּוֹן,
hayinu k'cholmim.	הָיִינוּ כְּחוֹלְמִים.
Az y'malei s'chok pinu,	אָז יִמָּלֵא שְׂחוֹק פִּינוּ
ul'shoneinu rinah.	וּלְשׁוֹנֵנוּ רִנָּה.
Az yomru vagoyim:	אָז יֹאמְרוּ בַגּוֹיִם:
Higdil Adonai laasot im eileh.	הִגְדִּיל יְיָ לַעֲשׂוֹת עִם־אֵלֶּה.
Higdil Adonai laasot imanu,	הִגְדִּיל יְיָ לַעֲשׂוֹת עִמָּנוּ,
hayinu s'meichim!	הָיִינוּ שְׂמֵחִים!
Shuvah Adonai et sh'viteinu	שׁוּבָה יְיָ אֶת־שְׁבִיתֵנוּ
kaafikim banegev	כַּאֲפִיקִים בַּנֶּגֶב
Hazorim b'dimah b'rinah	הַזֹּרְעִים בְּדִמְעָה בְּרִנָּה
yiktzoru.	יִקְצֹרוּ.
Haloch yeileich u'vacho,	הָלוֹךְ יֵלֵךְ וּבָכֹה
nosei meshech hazara,	נֹשֵׂא מֶשֶׁךְ־הַזָּרַע,
bo yavo v'rinah nosei alumotav.	בֹּא־יָבוֹא בְרִנָּה נֹשֵׂא אֲלֻמֹתָיו

A PILGRIM SONG: When God restores the exiles to Zion, it will seem like a dream. Our mouths will fill with laughter, our tongues with joyful song. They will say among the nations: God has done great things for them. Yes, God is doing great things for us, and we are joyful. Restore our fortunes, O God, as streams revive the desert. Then those who have sown in tears shall reap in joy. Those who go forth weeping, carrying bags of seeds, shall come home with shouts of joy, bearing their sheaves. [Psalm 126]

LEADER

Chaveirim v'chaveirot n'vareich.　　　　חֲבֵרִים וְחַבֵרוֹת נְבָרֵךְ.

Let us praise God.

ALL

Y'hi shem Adonai m'vorach　　　　יְהִי שֵׁם יְיָ מְבֹרָךְ
mei-atah v'ad olam!　　　　מֵעַתָּה וְעַד עוֹלָם.

Praised be the name of God, now and for ever!.

LEADER

Y'hi shem Adonai m'vorach　　　　יְהִי שֵׁם יְיָ מְבֹרָךְ
mei-atah v'ad olam!　　　　מֵעַתָּה וְעַד עוֹלָם.

Praised be the name of God, now and for ever!.

Birshut chaveirai v'rabotai n'vareich　　בִּרְשׁוּת חֲבֵרַי וְרַבּוֹתַי נְבָרֵךְ
Eloheinu she-achalnu mishelo.　　אֱלֹהֵינוּ שֶׁאָכַלְנוּ מִשֶּׁלוֹ.

Priased be our God, of whose abundance we have eaten.

ALL

Baruch Eloheinu she-achalnu　　　　בָּרוּךְ אֱלֹהֵינוּ שֶׁאָכַלְנוּ
mishelo uvtuvo chayinu.　　　　מִשֶּׁלוֹ וּבְטוּבוֹ חָיִינוּ.

Praised be, our God, of whose abundance we have eaten,
and by whose goodness we live.

◀ 176 ▶

Baruch Eloheinu she-achalnu   בָּרוּךְ אֱלֹהֵינוּ שֶׁאָכַלְנוּ

mishelo uvtuvo chayinu.   מִשֶּׁלוֹ וּבְטוּבוֹ חָיִינוּ.

Baruch Hu, uvaruch sh'mo.   בָּרוּךְ הוּא וּבָרוּךְ שְׁמוֹ.

Praised be, our God, of whose abundance we have eaten,
and by whose goodness we live. Praised be the Eternal God!

ALL

Baruch atah Adonai,   בָּרוּךְ אַתָּה יְיָ

Eloheinu Melech haolam   אֱלֹהֵינוּ מֶלֶךְ הָעוֹלָם

hazan et haolam kulo b'tuvo   הַזָּן אֶת הָעוֹלָם כֻּלּוֹ בְּטוּבוֹ

b'chein b'chesed uvrachamim,   בְּחֵן בְּחֶסֶד וּבְרַחֲמִים,

Hu notein lechem l'chol basar,   הוּא נוֹתֵן לֶחֶם לְכָל-בָּשָׂר,

ki l'olam chasdo.   כִּי לְעוֹלָם חַסְדּוֹ.

Uvtuvo hagadol tamid lo chasar   וּבְטוּבוֹ הַגָּדוֹל תָּמִיד לֹא חָסַר

lanu v'al yechsar lanu mazon   לָנוּ וְאַל יֶחְסַר-לָנוּ מָזוֹן

l'olam va-ed.   לְעוֹלָם וָעֶד.

Baavur sh'mo hagadol   בַּעֲבוּר שְׁמוֹ הַגָּדוֹל

ki hu El zan umfarneis lakol   כִּי הוּא אֵל זָן וּמְפַרְנֵס לַכָּל

umeitiv lakol umeichin mazon   וּמֵטִיב לַכָּל וּמֵכִין מָזוֹן

l'chol b'riyotav asher bara.   לְכָל-בְּרִיּוֹתָיו אֲשֶׁר בָּרָא.

Baruch atah Adonai,   בָּרוּךְ אַתָּה יְיָ,

hazan et hakol.   הַזָּן אֶת הַכֹּל.

Sovereign God of the universe, we praise You: Your goodness sustains the
world. You are the God of grace, love, and compassion, the source of bread
for all who live—for Your love is everlasting. In Your great goodness we need
never lack for food; You provide food enough for all. We praise You, O God,
Source of food for all who live.

(OPTIONAL)

Nodeh l'cha Adonai Eloheinu   נוֹדֶה לְךָ יְיָ אֱלֹהֵינוּ

al shehinchalta laavoteinu   עַל שֶׁהִנְחַלְתָּ לַאֲבוֹתֵינוּ

eretz chemdah tovah ur'chavah,	אֶרֶץ חֶמְדָּה טוֹבָה וּרְחָבָה,
v'al shehotzeitanu mei-Eretz	וְעַל שֶׁהוֹצֵאתָנוּ מֵאֶרֶץ
Mitzrayim v'al b'ritcha	מִצְרַיִם וְעַל בְּרִיתְךָ
shechatamta bilvaveinu,	שֶׁחָתַמְתָּ בִּלְבָבֵנוּ
v'al toratcha shelimadtanu,	וְעַל תּוֹרָתְךָ שֶׁלִּמַּדְתָּנוּ,
v'al chukecha shehodatanu,	וְעַל חֻקֶּיךָ שֶׁהוֹדַעְתָּנוּ,
v'al chayim, chein vachesed	וְעַל חַיִּים, חֵן וָחֶסֶד
shechonantanu, v'al achilat	שֶׁחוֹנַנְתָּנוּ וְעַל אֲכִילַת
mazon she-atah zan umfarneis	מָזוֹן שָׁאַתָּה זָן וּמְפַרְנֵס
otanu tamid, b'chol yom	אוֹתָנוּ תָּמִיד, בְּכָל-יוֹם
uv'chol eit uv'chol shaah.	וּבְכָל-עֵת וּבְכָל-שָׁעָה.

For this good earth that You have entrusted to our mothers and fathers, and to us; for our deliverance from bondage; for the covenant You have sealed in our hearts; for Your life-giving love and grace; for Torah, our ways of life, and for the food that sustains us day by day, we give You thanks.

(OPTIONAL)

V'al hakol Adonai Eloheinu	וְעַל הַכֹּל יְיָ אֱלֹהֵינוּ
anachnu modim lach	אֲנַחְנוּ מוֹדִים לָךְ,
um'varchim otach.	וּמְבָרְכִים אוֹתָךְ.
Yitbarach shimcha b'fi kol chai	יִתְבָּרַךְ שִׁמְךָ בְּפִי כָּל-חַי
tamid l'olam va-ed, kakatuv	תָּמִיד לְעוֹלָם וָעֶד, כַּכָּתוּב
v'achalta v'savata uveirachta	וְאָכַלְתָּ וְשָׂבָעְתָּ וּבֵרַכְתָּ
et Adonai Elohecha al haaretz	אֶת-יְיָ אֱלֹהֶיךָ עַל הָאָרֶץ
hatovah asher natan lach.	הַטּוֹבָה אֲשֶׁר נָתַן לָךְ.
Baruch atah Adonai, al haaretz	בָּרוּךְ אַתָּה יְיָ, עַל הָאָרֶץ
v'al hamazon.	וְעַל הַמָּזוֹן.

For all this we thank You. Let Your praise ever be on the lips of all who live, as it is written: "When you have eaten and are satisfied, give praise to your God who has given you this good earth." We praise You, O God, for the earth, and for its sustenance. Amen.

Racheim Adonai Eloheinu	רַחֵם יְיָ אֱלֹהֵינוּ
al Yisrael amecha	עַל יִשְׂרָאֵל עַמֶּךָ,
v'al Y'rushalayim irecha	וְעַל יְרוּשָׁלַיִם עִירֶךָ,
v'al Tziyon mishkan k'vodecha	וְעַל צִיּוֹן מִשְׁכַּן כְּבוֹדֶךָ
Eloheinu avinu, imeinu,	אֱלֹהֵינוּ אָבִינוּ, אִמֵּנוּ
r'einu zuneinu parn'seinu	רְעֵנוּ זוּנֵנוּ, פַּרְנְסֵנוּ
v'chalk'leinu v'harvicheinu	וְכַלְכְּלֵנוּ וְהַרְוִיחֵנוּ,
v'harvach lanu Adonai Eloheinu	וְהַרְוַח־לָנוּ, יְיָ אֱלֹהֵינוּ
m'heira mikol tzaroteinu.	מְהֵרָה מִכָּל־צָרוֹתֵינוּ.
V'na al tatzricheinu,	וְנָא עַל תַּצְרִיכֵנוּ,
Adonai Eloheinu lo lidei matnat	יְיָ אֱלֹהֵינוּ, לֹא לִידֵי מַתְּנַת
basar vadam v'lo lidei halvaatam,	בָּשָׂר וָדָם וְלֹא לִידֵי הַלְוָאָתָם,
ki im l'yadcha hamlei-ah	כִּי אִם לְיָדְךָ הַמְּלֵאָה
hap'tucha hak'dosha v'harchavah	הַפְּתוּחָה הַקְּדוֹשָׁה וְהָרְחָבָה,
shelo neivosh v'lo nikaleim	שֶׁלֹּא נֵבוֹשׁ וְלֹא נִכָּלֵם
l'olam va-ed.	לְעוֹלָם וָעֶד.

Eternal God, Source of our being, show compassion for Israel Your people, Jerusalem Your city, and Zion, the ancient dwelling-place of Your glory. Guide and sustain us in all our habitations, and be a help to us in all our troubles. May we ever be able to help ourselves and one another, even as we rely on Your open and generous bounty.

ALL

Uv'nei Y'rushalayim ir hakodesh	וּבְנֵה יְרוּשָׁלַיִם עִיר הַקֹּדֶשׁ
bimheira v'yameinu.	בִּמְהֵרָה בְיָמֵינוּ.
Baruch atah Adonai,	בָּרוּךְ אַתָּה יְיָ,
bone v'rachamav Y'rushalayim	בּוֹנֵה בְרַחֲמָיו יְרוּשָׁלָיִם.
Amen.	אָמֵן.

Let Jerusalem, the holy city, be renewed in our time. We praise You, O God, who in compassion rebuilds Jerusalem. Amen.

Baruch atah Adonai,	בָּרוּךְ אַתָּה יְיָ,
Eloheinu Melech haolam,	אֱלֹהֵינוּ מֶלֶךְ הָעוֹלָם,
haEl avinu malkeinu, adireinu,	הָאֵל אָבִינוּ מַלְכֵּנוּ, אַדִּירֵנוּ,
boreinu, go-aleinu, yotzreinu,	בּוֹרְאֵנוּ, גּוֹאֲלֵנוּ,יוֹצְרֵנוּ,
k'dosheinu, k'dosh Ya'akov	קְדוֹשֵׁנוּ, קְדוֹשׁ יַעֲקֹב,
ro-einu, ro-ei Yisrael,	רוֹעֵנוּ, רוֹעֵה יִשְׂרָאֵל,
hamelech hatov v'hameitiv lakol	הַמֶּלֶךְ הַטּוֹב וְהַמֵּיטִיב לַכֹּל.
sheb'chol yom vayom Hu heitiv,	שֶׁבְּכָל-יוֹם וָיוֹם הוּא הֵטִיב,
Hu meitiv, Hu yeitiv lanu,	הוּא מֵטִיב, הוּא יֵטִיב לָנוּ.
Hu g'malanu, Hu gomleinu,	הוּא גְמָלָנוּ, הוּא גוֹמְלֵנוּ,
Hu yigmaleinu laad,	הוּא יִגְמְלֵנוּ לָעַד,
l'chein l'chesed ul'rachamim,	לְחֵן לְחֶסֶד וּלְרַחֲמִים,
ul'revach hatzalah v'hatzlachah,	וּלְרֶוַח, הַצָּלָה וְהַצְלָחָה,
b'rachah vishuah, nechamah,	בְּרָכָה וִישׁוּעָה, נֶחָמָה,
parnasah, v'chalkalah,	פַּרְנָסָה וְכַלְכָּלָה,
v'rachamim v'chayim, v'shalom,	וְרַחֲמִים וְחַיִּים וְשָׁלוֹם,
v'chol tov, umikol tov	וְכָל-טוֹב, וּמִכָּל-טוֹב
al y'chasreinu.	אַל-יְחַסְּרֵנוּ.

We praise You, divine Parent of Israel, Source of liberating power and vision, of all that is holy and good. You have shown us love and kindness always; day by day You grant us grace and compassion, deliverance and freedom, prosperity and blessing, life and peace.

Harachaman, Hu y'vareich et-   -הָרַחֲמָן הוּא יְבָרֵךְ אֶת

Select the appropriate one . . .

GROOM AND BRIDE

hechatan v'et hakallah   הֶחָתָן וְאֶת-הַכַּלָּה

GROOM AND GROOM

hechatan v'et hechatan   הֶחָתָן וְאֶת-הֶחָתָן

BRIDE AND BRIDE

hakallah v'et hakallah   הַכַּלָּה וְאֶת-הַכַּלָּה

LOVING COMPANIONS (MALE OR MIXED GENDER)

harei-im haahuvim   הָרֵעִים הָאֲהוּבִים

LOVING COMPANIONS (FEMALE)

harei-ot haahuvot   הָרֵעוֹת הָאֲהוּבוֹת

Continue . . .

et kol hayoshvim po,	אֶת-כָּל הַיּוֹשְׁבִים פֹּה,
otanu v'et kol asher lanu,	אוֹתָנוּ וְאֶת-כָּל-אֲשֶׁר לָנוּ,
k'mo shenitbarchu avoteinu	כְּמוֹ שֶׁנִּתְבָּרְכוּ אֲבוֹתֵינוּ,
Avraham, Yitzchak, v'Yaakov,	אַבְרָהָם, יִצְחָק, וְיַעֲקֹב,
v'imoteinu, Sarah, Rivkah,	וְאִמּוֹתֵינוּ, שָׂרָה, רִבְקָה,
Leah, v'Rachel	לֵאָה וְרָחֵל,
kein y'vareich otanu	כֵּן יְבָרֵךְ אוֹתָנוּ
kulanu yachad,	כֻּלָּנוּ יַחַד,
bivrachah sh'leimah, v'nomar:	בִּבְרָכָה שְׁלֵמָה, וְנֹאמַר
Amen.	אָמֵן.

Merciful One, bless the . . . groom and bride / groom and groom / bride and bride / loving companions . . . and all those seated here, us and all our dear ones, as You blessed our ancestors, Abraham, Isaac, and Jacob; Sarah, Rebekah, Leah, and Rachel, so bless us, one and all; and let us say: Amen.

ALL

Oseh shalom bimromav	עוֹשֶׂה שָׁלוֹם בִּמְרוֹמָיו
Hu yaaseh shalom aleinu	הוּא יַעֲשֶׂה שָׁלוֹם עָלֵינוּ
v'al kol Yisrael,	וְעַל כָּל יִשְׂרָאֵל
v'al kol yoshvei teiveil	וְעַל כָּל-יוֹשְׁבֵי תֵבֵל
v'imru: Amen.	וְאִמְרוּ אָמֵן.

May the Source of perfect peace grant peace to us, to all Israel,
and to all the world.

Appendix VIII

Resources in the Reform Movement

Central Conference of American Rabbis
E-mail: info@ccarnet.org
Web: www.ccarnet.org
Phone: 1-800-935-CCAR
(For information about Reform rabbis in your area)

American Conference of Cantors
Phone: 516-239-3650
(For information about Reform Cantors in your area)

Union of American Hebrew Congregations
E-mail: uahc.org (national)
Web: www.uahc.org
Phone   212-650-4000 (national)
(For information about Reform congregations and programs in your area, and information about the Jewish calendar)

Transcontinental Music Publications
Internet: www.eTranscon.com
Phone: 800-455-5223
(For sheet music and CD's for Jewish weddings)